"At a time when youth spo
parents pushing their kids
lenges moms and dads to
remember that, win or lose, sports can play a p...
ment of our children's character. In *More Than the Score*, Pat shows us what it looks like to parent our children wisely through their sporting endeavors."

Jim Daly
President, Focus on the Family

"Pat Combs provides great insights for coaching, parenting, and life in *More Than the Score*. Weaving together timeless principles from farming, sports, and Biblical principles, Pat offers great perspective on the right way to play in any game or endeavor."

Tim Tassopoulos
President & COO, Chick-fil-A, Inc.

"As a Mom of a competitive athlete, *More Than the Score* resonates with me, big time! In addition, in my role at Jockey International, and because I was adopted myself, I've been a passionate advocate for adoption and helping families find their way through our Jockey Being Family initiative. I've seen firsthand the powerful impact that a loving family can have on a child. It's the best place on earth to grow our next generation of strong leaders. This book is a game changer for any dad, mom or coach who wants to help children have a positive impact on and off the field. Pat is a personal friend of mine, and I'm thrilled he's on a mission to help parents redeem youth sports and strengthen families. I encourage you to read the book and put it into practice!"

Debra S. Waller
Chairman & CEO of Jockey International, Inc.
Founder of Jockey Being Family

"In his book *More Than the Score*, Pat Combs tackles important issues. As a professional athlete, Combs provides an inside look at a world that fascinates many Americans. He also discusses ways to help kids be successful by addressing every parent's top priority. Laced with interesting stories, practical advice, and timeless wisdom, this book will inspire you to view sports differently and take your parenting to a new level."

Richard Blackaby
President, Blackaby Ministries International
Co-author of Experiencing God *and* Experiencing God at Home

"Like so many other things in life, sports can be a huge positive or a huge negative, a crucible for character formation or an idol of destruction. Those who venture into the sports world with their children need the sort of wisdom you'll find in this book."

John Stonestreet
President, the Chuck Colson Center for Christian Worldview

"Pat's book, *More Than the Score*, will give parents and coaches practical tools they can use with young athletes. It's crucial that we help young men and women grow in character, virtue and responsibility. We must reverse the trend of hyper-competitive and high-pressure youth sports by helping them enjoy the game and learn valuable life skills along the way. Pat's book will help us do that!"

Mark Merrill
President, Family First and All Pro Dad

"Pat's experience, and thus, his advice in *More Than the Score* is a *must* read for anyone wanting to be the best parent and coach possible. This quick and powerful read will be one you will want to read all the way through. I will be sharing this book with everyone!"

Logan Stout
Best Selling Author, Speaker, Entrepreneur and Coach

"The game belongs to the kids, but Pat shows how parents can use the game to shape the character of their kids. Filled with honest stories and keen insights, *More Than the Score* serves as a gracious guide for parents seeking to use sports to develop the character of their kids. Instead of living vicariously through his kids on the field, Pat candidly shares how he allowed the field to shape his kids. I look up to Pat and have been blessed by Pat through his kids. They are men who have shaped me and continually motivate me to be a better man. The fields are white for harvest and it is time to play ball. I highly recommend *More Than the Score*, knowing you will be blessed by it and heaven will be more populated because of it."

Dr. J. Nick Pitts
Executive Director of the Institute for Global Engagement, Dallas Baptist University

"Our culture in America continues to grapple with increasing anger and character issues. We've become, in many ways, so focused on ourselves and our own agendas, that we don't reach out and connect with people around us. At its heart, this is a character issue and we need to help our young men and women see that there is a different way. Pat's book, *More Than the Score*, will help parents win at the larger game of shaping our nation for generations to come. For parents and coaches who care about the future of our country, this book will be a significant asset in their toolbox. Read this book now, for the sake of the next generation!"

Kevin Sorbo
Producer and Actor

"Raising children is a tremendous honor and responsibility. In *More Than the Score*, Pat Combs takes the reader through the real-life challenges of raising three active, athletic boys, from a godly perspective. This book teaches life-proven principles in real time and is written with humility, vulnerability and honesty. At the end of each section is "Digging Deeper," an opportunity to reflect on how to respond in both the good and difficult times. The book is introspective, personal, and well written, offering valuable wisdom to every parent. I give *More Than the Score* five stars!"

Tom Roy
President of SHEPHERD COACH NETWORK—www. shepherdcoachnetwork.com

"Wow! What a timely book for today's culture. As a former teammate, long-time friend, and current ministry partner, I can attest to the passion through which Pat lives life. His passion is evident in the pages of this book as he helps us discover our 'why' as parents, coaches, and influencers of today's youth. Pat is a proven role model who skillfully communicates godly principles and practical advice for this generation and generations to come. My only regret is that this book wasn't written 20 years ago when I was raising my children. Well done, Pat!"

Mickey Weston
Executive Director, Unlimited Potential Inc.

"*More Than the Score* really speaks to how Pat and Christina navigated through the noise and 'crowd think' that pulled at their three amazing sons and athletes. In the process, they found a way to turn their boys into men without losing family togetherness in the process. This book is a great roadmap for those parents who are trying to navigate the same route. I pray you are as successful as 'Pat's team' has been!"

Flip Flippen
Founder & Chairman, The Flippen Group
NY Times Best Selling Author of *The Flip Side*

Is your daughter/son playing youth sports? Are you a frequent "Yeller!" at the refs for bad calls? Are you a frequent "Yeller" at your daughter or son for what you perceive to be a lack of effort or making the wrong moves? Or would you say that the greatest values of youth sports are the building of character and teamwork—not just for your daughter or son but also for you the parent? If your answers are, "Yeah, sometimes. Yeah, sometimes." and, "Thanks for reminding me that it really is about building character and teamwork!", then this is a crucial book for you! My friend, Pat Combs' new book *More Than the Score* is a must-read for every parent whose daughter or son is playing youth sports. It contains over 300 questions that will help you successfully navigate your family's youth sports journey to arrive at the destinations of "Character-Built" and "Teamwork-Valued!"

Bob Tiede
Blogger at LeadingWithQuestions.com and author of *Great Leaders ASK Questions* and *Now That's a Great Question*

MORE
THAN
THE
SCORE

MORE THAN THE SCORE

HOW PARENTS AND COACHES CAN CULTIVATE VIRTUE IN YOUTH ATHLETES

PAT COMBS

MORE THAN THE SCORE

Trade Paperback ISBN 978-1-949856-25-5

e-Book ISBN 978-1-949856-26-2

Cover Design by Reba Cooke | www.rebareneedesign.com
General editing by Ryan Sanders

Published globally by Manhood Journey Press, an imprint of Manhood Journey, Inc., 212 Prestwick Place, Louisville, Kentucky 40243.

Manhood Journey and the Father & Son Circle Logo are both registered trademarks of Manhood Journey, Inc.

SPECIAL SALES
Copies of More Than the Score can be purchased at special quantity discounts when purchased in bulk by corporations, leagues, educational institutions and other special-interest groups. Contact the publisher for information at info@manhoodjourney.org.

DEDICATION

By far the biggest impact in my life is the love of my life, my beautiful bride of 30 years and counting, Christina. None of this happens without you! Carson, Conner and Casey are blessed with an amazing mom. You have sacrificed many of your own goals and desires to serve your family. I will always be grateful that God put us together!

To my sons, it has been so cool to be your dad. We've had a blast, haven't we? You have had a tremendous foundation built upon athletics. I am incredibly thankful the Lord blessed us with you guys. Some of my greatest days on this planet have occurred while I was coaching, teaching, mentoring and discipling you, my sons!

TABLE OF CONTENTS

FOREWORD

by Former MLB Pitcher Andy Pettitte

I surrendered my life to Jesus Christ at age eleven. My sister had attended a church in Deer Park, Texas, where I grew up. She became a Christ-follower, and she told me I needed to go hear what that was about. I went with her, met Jesus, and nothing has been the same since. Through my sister's invitation, Jesus changed my life forever.

That might seem an odd place to begin the foreword for my friend Pat Combs' book, but I really have to start there. My relationship with Jesus has shaped every decision I've made since that day. Nothing else even comes close.

Well, one thing might. Besides this event at eleven, the second greatest life-influencing encounter I had was with my girlfriend Laura Dunn in high school. I knew early on this was one special lady. Earlier this year, we celebrated our 27th wedding anniversary, and we've been blessed with four children, three sons and a daughter.

I met Jesus as a boy, and Laura as a teenager. I was especially fortunate in that Laura's family were deeply involved in ministry work. Her dad was a pastor and her brothers have held various church and ministry related roles. Their influence caused me to want to grow in my walk. Ever since my teen years, I've been surrounded by an extended family that's been a great influence on me.

I share all this to help you see something very clearly: from age eleven, I've seen God's hand on my life. Who I met, doors that opened, even the way he wired me mentally and physically was for a purpose and a plan that He clearly wanted to see play out in my life. I can't take credit for hardly any of it.

Now, I tried hard to use the skills and tools he gave me to the best of my ability. There was a ton of hard work in my baseball career that I could've tried to skip, but I leaned into those gifts and tried to make the best use of them. I didn't always succeed.

It's an odd thing. On one hand, I had this passion to serve Jesus and my wife (and now my kids) with all I had. But, at the same time, I was a competitor. I expected the best out of myself, and if I had a bad outing, I didn't just walk off the mound and wonder what might be for dinner later. I was angry and frustrated with myself, and sometimes, the nearest dugout wall or water cooler was going to feel it. I've seen that, "Uh-oh, stand back!" look on the face of my coaches and teammates more than once as I headed back to the dugout.

I'm not proud of that, but it was part of walking out my faith. I tried to be an example of both a strong competitor and a faithful Christ-follower. It wasn't easy. I got it wrong often. I had surrendered my life to Christ, but that didn't mean I'd been stripped of my competitive fire.

Having said that, I distinctly remember in my teen years making some decisions that put God above baseball. There were many times that I skipped a big tournament to attend a summer church camp. I almost never skipped church to play a game. I had a conviction that I needed to honor God, and He would take control of everything else. He was in control of my life, and He still is.

And, guess what? When you find a teenage boy who has conviction that God should be his focus, and not his sports or dating activities, do you know what you have? A walking miracle, that's what. Only God can do that in someone's heart, especially a young man's.

Even as an aggressive and competitive athlete, I just knew there was more to this life than simply winning games or getting noticed by a coach or scout. In this book, Pat makes the point that if you have talent, you will be found. I agree with him completely. I ended up getting noticed by a junior college, and after only one year there, was thrust into the fire of the minor leagues.

I realized that our current youth and high school sports scene is different. I've made some other choices as a dad of athletes that I might not have made twenty years ago. The landscape of our current select sports environment has shifted, and it's not as easy to skip things and make progress as an athlete.

However—I'm still convinced of this—we must put God above sports. We must love Jesus more than we love our careers (sports or otherwise). We need to surround ourselves with people who will reinforce those choices and help us stay on track. And, in the sports world, the higher you go, the more challenging it can become to walk out your faith.

I had my share of lonely times when I didn't want to join my playing buddies in their "evening activities." I was jabbed at, ignored, criticized and made fun of. It was no fun; but, it wasn't the end of the world either.

Especially in my early professional days, I would always come home to a supportive, faithful and encouraging wife, who kept me anchored and focused. Again, I knew this was God's way of providing the support I needed to follow His plan for my life.

When I was a pitcher, one of my goals was to "setup" a hitter. I would try to throw certain pitches early, so the batter might get off balance or expect a certain pitch later. Then, I'd try to outguess him and throw something he didn't see coming. You're probably too smart for that, but, so far, I've been doing the same thing to you. I want to "set you up." But in this case, I want to help you, not have you strike out.

The setup is this: God has been actively influencing my life since I was born. None of my experiences were random, He was trying to get my attention and help me live a fruitful life since the day I walked into that church with my sister.

He is doing the same thing to you. And He wants to do the same thing through you. You may be a parent, a coach, or both. You picked up this book because there's something about how you're influencing the children in your life—yours or those you're coaching—that you know is more important than wins and losses. But, you may not be sure what that is.

It's Jesus. It's having a saving, intimate, personal relationship with a God who loves you so much that He sent His Son to die for you. That's the "only pitch" I want to give you. And, unlike my days on the mound, I want to serve this one up nice and easy so you can smash it to kingdom come.

God wants to use you as an influence on the lives of some young people. They might live under your roof, or they might live across town. You can help these kids find what really matters. That's not a D-1 scholarship or a pro sports contract. Even the best of those things will one day turn to dust.

The only thing that really matters is whether these kids learn how to love, trust and follow Jesus. And I would say, this is especially true for those of them who do "make it" to the big leagues. If they don't have a foundation in Christ, pro sports will eat them alive.

I hope this book helps you do something as a parent or coach when it comes to sports. Relax. Back off a bit. Chill out. The odds are your children will not play at a professional level, and I'm right there with you. My oldest son has had four elbow surgeries, and he knows that he will not be playing professional sports for his career.

So, our job as parents is to prepare our kids for the road ahead. We need to set the chase of a big-time contract or scholarship aside and focus on the character and priorities our kids are developing. We need to help them see that Jesus Christ is the way, the truth and the life. We need to help them find faithful spouses, stay in God's word, and walk in a worthy manner. It's a daily struggle, and I'm walking it out as a parent like you are.

I want my children to love Jesus more than anything, and I want them each to find spouses who feel the same way. Beyond the fame and fortune of pro sports, that's what really matters.

I hope you will join me in reading this book and putting it into practice. The lives of our children and the other young men and women we're influencing will never be the same. Go out into those fields and reap a harvest!

Andy Pettitte
Houston, TX

INTRODUCTION

I was born to love the game of baseball. It's almost as if I didn't even have a choice.

I grew up in a sports-loving family in Houston, Texas. My room was full of Houston sports memorabilia: Astros posters, Oilers pennants (the "Luv Ya Blue" days), and Rockets memorabilia. The 1970's was a great time to be a sports fan. It was a day when children could ride their bicycles to evening practices and most streets were filled with kids playing stick ball and touch football games. Recreation leagues were the happening place for young athletes. It seemed every neighborhood child was on a sports team. The skill-level mattered much less than it does today. We simply wanted to be a part of a team.

One event stands out in my memory. My grandfather and I drove to the Sharpstown Little League field to sign up for spring baseball in Houston one fine Saturday in 1974. I'll never forget this day, mainly because it was so disappointing.

I desperately wanted to wrestle or box. When my granddad (Big Pop) said he was taking me to sign up for Little League baseball, I cried. Little did I know, this particular Saturday would set me on a life-changing journey. As God and my granddad would have it, this unwanted trek eventually led to my pitching for Rice University (1986), Baylor University (1987-88), the USA National Baseball team (1987-88), the Philadelphia Phillies (1989-95), and the Milwaukee Brewers (1995-96). Little did I know.

I became one of the .002 percent of Little League baseball players who made it to the Big Leagues. Only one half of one percent of high school players are drafted by a Major League Baseball (MLB) team; far fewer will ever take the field. Only 11 in 100 NCAA baseball players receive a chance to play at the next level in professional baseball.

God chose to bless me with some athletic ability and then by allowing the right doors to open at the right time. His hand on my life was evident. It was an absolute blast, and I'm grateful for the ability and opportunities He brought to me. There are so many great memories that I can't recall all of them. I wake up every day remembering my time in baseball as a precious gift.

This is especially true when I consider that it was something which took two decades to fully develop, only to have it end almost overnight.

Like many athletes, injury cut my career short. I exited the game I loved at the ripe old age of 30. My professional career started with a bang. I became the first player in baseball history who, in his first professional season, touched every level of the Minor Leagues (A, AA, AAA), all the way up to the Major Leagues in the same year. I got the call up to the big dance in September of 1989. In 1991, Andrew Jones of the Atlanta Braves had the same experience.

To this day, we're still the only two players who had such a hot start to their professional baseball careers in that way. It's pretty cool to have your name mentioned as part of an answer to an occasional baseball trivia question.

My call-up started a three-year run in the Major Leagues. I wish it could've been longer, but injuries to my pitching arm sent me back down into the Philadelphia Phillies' minor league system. I battled through injuries for four seasons. My career ended, disappointingly, in the Milwaukee Brewers farm system in 1996. I was cut from the Brewers that spring, and it was time to put my playing days in the rearview mirror.

The lead-up to my professional playing days was no less exciting. One of the great highlights of my time in amateur baseball came in the Summers of 1987 and 1988. I was fortunate enough to be allowed to represent the United States on our National baseball team. Our 1988 squad became the first ever gold medal baseball team in US Olympic history.

Team USA took us all over the planet those two summers. We were the first American team to visit Havana, Cuba, in 27 years. We traveled to Japan and played in major cities against a talented Japanese Olympic team. The 1987 tour ended in the World Baseball Championships in Italy, where we lost in a controversial finish to the Cubans. We played in more than 40 cities.

Some of my greatest memories in baseball came during this time. I was coached by some of the greatest college baseball coaches of all time. Coaches like Ron Frazier (Miami), Mark Marquess (Stanford), Skip Bertman (LSU), and Ron Polk (Mississippi State). Our team boasted baseball greats like Jim Abbott, Andy Benes, Charlie Nagy, Tino Martinez, Scott Servais, and Tom Goodwin. The gold medal was a bonus on top of being led by and playing alongside such talented teammates.

I'm not sharing these stories just so you can stroll down memory lane with me or to show off my baseball resume. I want you to see something hidden inside my story.

First, did I enjoy my baseball career? Yes, without a doubt. But, was it a grind? Absolutely! Every professional athlete will tell you that. It's not just about talent, travel, or teammates. It's about the work, the challenges, and the setbacks.

The players who make it to the top levels must work hard to get there. They arrive in part because they're driven individuals. But, once they get there, they quickly realize how unbelievably difficult it is to stick at the highest level of their profession! Every. Single. Day.

We quickly understand that our performance depends on our bodies, and a minor injury can sideline the most talented player. This is the risk we signed up for to play such a great game. We realize that, in one sense, we're just a number. A hired hand who can disappear any moment. There's always someone on deck waiting to take our place.

That's life in professional sports. In many ways, it can be the glamorous, wealth-building profession most think it is. But, in other ways that usually go unnoticed, life as a professional athlete is difficult. It's filled with constant fears of not measuring up, getting hurt, or being let go. You live with a mindset characterized by constant risk. This doesn't work well for your family. The divorce rate ranges from 60 to 80 percent for professional athlete couples within two years of leaving the game*. That's a staggering number of wrecked families, confused children, and broken lives.

At this point, maybe you're rethinking your goals for your child to play professional sports! I'm not trying to paint a bleak picture. I don't want to discourage you or any young athlete from pursuing their dreams of making it to the big stage.

Yet, my hope is that you will consider all the costs. You should know what a career in professional sports may cost your child and your family so you can make the wisest decisions.

This is why I believe my story is really about *your story*.

I will use it as a backdrop for *More Than the Score* just so you might gain hope and help to raise your children in a way that yields great fruit. This is why I wanted to frame my comments in the context of a farming metaphor. I think this will help you see the ideas more clearly and apply them more quickly to your own life, because, this book is not about me. It's about you. Your family. The children you're raising or the young men and women you're coaching.

My heart's desire is to spur your family on to enjoy the journey that sports can take you on. As we walk these fields together, I want you to see sports for what they really are: a training ground. This training ground is not just meant to teach our children how to drill home runs, make baskets or drive the ball into the end zone. We

---

*Lariviere, David, *Forbes*. "Divorce, Not Domestic Violence, Is Biggest Issue at Home for Professional Athletes". August 15, 2014. *https://www.forbes.com/sites/davidlariviere/2014/08/15/divorce-not-domestic-violence-is-biggest-issue-at-home-for-professional-athletes/*

must be after something more than *just* the score. I think this "something" can best be described as a harvest.

I hope you glean some insights and ideas as you read these pages. Perhaps my experience as a professional athlete will be instructive for you and your family as you navigate the sports world. But more importantly, I hope it inspires you to be a thoughtful and engaged parent to your children or a more intentional coach to those entrusted to you.

My most important role in life was not as a major league pitcher. It was, and is, being a godly husband to my wife and father to my boys. And both are jobs I botched frequently. Christina could fill volumes with all the dumb stuff I did. Even so, we tried hard to be great parents and to do things right. We were blessed with lots of help over the years. I hope this book will be an encouragement and resource to you—wherever you are in the journey—to raise up your young athlete.

So far, I've enjoyed a life of exciting opportunity mixed with plenty of heartache and adversity. Some decisions worked out well and yielded great fruit. Other choices resulted in loss and damage. It's probably a lot like yours in that way.

I can't think of youth sports and parenting and not think of fields. Fields that are either ripe for harvest or ones that are barren and dry. The Bible speaks a lot about agriculture and gives us a beautiful metaphor for personal growth in the sowing and reaping process. My dear friend, Cal VanSingel, is intimately acquainted with sowing and reaping.

Cal is a farmer. He happens to be one of the most gracious men I know. I once enjoyed a long visit to his third-generation farm located on 1,500 acres in Grant, Michigan. It's one of the longest-running private family farms in the country. He gave me the royal treatment: a personal tour in his very own pickup truck. He showed me where they grow onions, carrots, parsnips, and potatoes.

Maybe you're like me and don't know much about farming. Well, it's quite the education. From a biblical perspective, knowing more about farming helps bring to life many of the verses that speak of growth and development. Across the acres that Cal and his family tend, the laws of sowing and reaping came to life for me. I could literally see the principles springing out of the ground as I stood at the top of a hill where Cal's house is located. From that perch, I gazed out and surveyed his entire farming operation. It's an incredible view.

I visited in the Summer. This is a time when the fields are still months from being harvested and the workers are focused on keeping the fields in prime condition as the crops are growing. Cal and his family were busy fixing the irrigation systems, working on their equipment, spraying for weeds, cleaning the barns and trying to get ahead of whatever could go wrong.

Isn't this idea of harvesting exactly what we're doing with our children? We stand at the door and see our children walk in from a long day at school or the ballfields. We take those little seeds of potential and plant the character and ideas that will best serve them in life.

This is the heart of the book you're holding. When we lead young men and women in sports endeavors, we must be after something more than just what happens on the scoreboard. We must view the whole system—the games, the practices, the locker room talks, the parent meetings—as a giant farmland, just waiting to yield a bountiful harvest. When we view ourselves as the parent-farmer in this equation, we get a clear picture of what it means to sow, tend, and reap a harvest of virtue, character and integrity. This is the maturation process we oversee in the hearts and minds of young people.

We continue to work hard to water and nurture that growth, while leveraging sports to help along the way. Sometimes, we intervene when something breaks down. Once in a while, when we can, we help them clean up the mess and help them learn from the mistake.

The ultimate goal is to prepare them for the day when they graduate and are producing their own fruit. We know unexpected challenges will come into their lives. The storms of life will gather and try to flood the harvest. Or the hot sun will scorch their lives and try to ruin any hopes of a fruitful crop. Are they ready? Will they have the skills to persevere and grind through what is ahead?

Parents and coaches are under immense pressure to get this right. A lot is riding on our choices. We are seeing sports culture change rapidly and we parents need to take responsibility. Our role shouldn't be to chase trophies on weekends or ensure our own children get the most playing time. We need to see the long game here.

We have a tremendous opportunity with our children and grandchildren. Think about the current crop of leaders in business, government, and education. Many honed their leadership skills through athletic competition. Why? Because that's often where children get challenged, pushed, and encouraged to explore the limits of their gifts. They learn incredible life skills that shape them forever. This only happens when we, their guides, direct them well and instill the right character along the way.

If we teach our children and players that they can and should live for something more than the score, they will grow into fruitful young men and women. These seeds planted will produce a rich harvest.

In the pages which follow, I'll share my experience—as a competitor, husband, and a dad. I'll weave in ideas and values that worked for us. I'll also share those that didn't! We made some mistakes along the way. But I trust you'll see we started with a solid perspective. We had God-honoring goals and a purpose beyond winning games. Looking back, I can honestly hang my cap on this: our ultimate goal wasn't simply to collect trophies. It was to build champions on and off the field.

May this book remind us of three very important truths. First, the fields—the hearts and minds of our children—are truly ripe for the harvest. Second, most of that fruit we pull in will be harvested off the field—not on it. Third, apart from God, we can do nothing.

Let's help our children and players live for *More Than the Score!*

Pat Combs
Southlake, Texas
September 2020

SECTION ONE

BEING THE PARENT FARMER

"The Lord God took the man and placed him in the garden of Eden to work it and watch over it."
Genesis 2:15

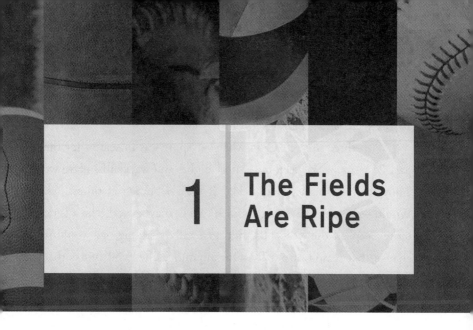

1 | The Fields Are Ripe

Youth sports can set us on an incredible journey filled with abundant blessings and joy. It can create a strong foundation of growth in our children. Looking back, I can see that my family has benefited tremendously from athletics. Which is comforting, since we've given huge chunks of our lives to sports.

Christina and I recently took a stroll down memory lane and compiled an alarming statistic. Over the course of our marriage, we've spent roughly 20 percent of our waking hours in some sports-related capacity: at fields or arenas for various reasons, driving to practices or games, watching the games, broadcasting games, and coaching.

We invested our time in this way because we realized that we had a special opportunity as parents to model lives of virtue for our children. Youth sports allowed us a unique time and place for doing that. But, as ripe as the fields were, my wife and I realized that fruit would only grow if we shared the same goals. We came to understand that success isn't about the scoreboard—it's about character growth.

We grew in our resolve over time with a fervent desire to honor God as parents, coaches and players of the game.

With three sons active in whatever sport was in season for the past 22 years, we've been busy most nights and weekends. Have we enjoyed it? Without a doubt! Has it been a burden at times? Yes! Would we change anything about it? Well, maybe we'd take a little more sleep on the weekends. But, generally speaking, we wouldn't change that season of our lives for anything. The good things that sports brought into our lives were so numerous they'd be hard to quantify. We can now stand back and celebrate the blessings we enjoyed as our boys participated over the years.

I believe one of the most important questions we can answer is, "Why are we spending our treasured time playing these sports?" If we can answer this question well, it becomes our barometer and compass. Our why helps define our purpose, and that helps us identify the real wins and losses, those beyond the scoreboard.

Our family's answer to why youth sports is simple. First, we enjoy sports. Well, wait, I should clarify something. I live and breathe sports, and my beautiful bride tolerates them. Unless, of course, her children are playing, then the Mom-Fan comes out big time! Over the years, though, we each realized that it's our job as parent-farmers to work and watch over our children in every area of their lives, much like a farmer tends the fields and keeps a keen eye on his crops. In particular, we felt we could do this well by being deeply engaged in their athletic endeavors.

Growing up as an athlete and competing at the highest levels, I experienced the greatest benefits that sports can offer. Yet, it came with some costs. My wife has always loved watching Carson, Conner, and Casey compete. However, she's also mentioned that there were times when she didn't appreciate how sports took me away from our family.

So, as a family, we needed to know our why, especially if we were going to devote so much time to this area of our lives. Our family's reason for diving into sports eventually moved far beyond just our love, passion, and enjoyment of the game. We came to recognize the many benefits of our children's involvement in athletics.

If our family's sports-time calculation is anything like yours—spending 20 percent of our waking hours participating in some sport—we knew how important it was for us to be united in our why. We sensed those times when we weren't aligned, and we knew we should make some adjustments. When we didn't have alignment in our purpose, we needed to stop, take a breath, hit our knees in prayer, and get on the same page. If sports were going to gobble up so much of our nights and weekends, we needed to agree on the why.

Clearly, getting on the same page is only part of the battle. If both mom and dad are unified in the idea that "our child will be a multi-millionaire hall of famer," that's equally as destructive. Our goal needs to be unity within an objective that honors God. If you are a single mom or dad, there may be additional challenges to unify regarding your children in sports, but hopefully there can be agreement about the best interests of your children. There is a tremendous encouragement in Psalm 133:1-3, ". . . when God's people live together in unity . . . the LORD bestows his blessing, even life forevermore." (NIV)

Our shared perspective about youth sports as it relates to our children is this: Christina and I feel that sports—when used correctly—are a tremendous tool to help shape our children into hard working, dedicated young men and women. The opportunities to learn the values of teamwork, discipline, responsibility, competing hard, how to win, and how to be graceful in defeat are endless. Above all, we wanted them to learn how to be great people, respect authority, and approach the game with passion.

We have a responsibility, as parents, to love our children well and to train them up. Proverbs 22:6 makes it clear that we are to, "Train up a child in the way he should go; even when he is old, he will not depart from it." Most importantly, we wanted our sons to honor God with their talents and have a relationship with Him. Everything else would be icing on the cake.

If you asked me today, "Did you ever dream of your children playing professional sports?" my honest answer would be, "Yes." Of course, I had dreams of my children having an opportunity to do what I did. But also, knowing what I know, I thought many times that I'd be just as glad if professional sports didn't happen for them. We'll save that for later in this book.

Since our children were toddlers, my perspective has been, "God, please mold and make these boys into the men *You want them to become*. Use them to impact the world in mighty ways. Above all, God, I want my sons to be the best they can be, for You. Help me be the best dad I can be. Help me to love their mother with all my heart, so they can see how a godly man should honor his wife. Please help me to learn how to protect, guide, and develop my sons—so they can fulfill the calling You place on their lives."

These prayers turned into goals we made as a family. We regularly worked with our sons to create goals, particularly ones related to their sports efforts. Once we all knew what we wanted to accomplish, our role as parents was to support and encourage.

My eldest son, Carson, developed a love for ice hockey and we did our best to support him. I didn't know squat about hockey, but I picked up the concepts and ideas as I hung around the game. Even though hockey was not my cup of tea, I wanted Carson to have a great experience and enjoy the game. We had no idea where hockey would lead him, especially being in Texas. As you might imagine, there aren't a lot of frozen bodies of water here.

Yet, he loved the sport and we eventually fell in love watching him play it. Today, it's one of my favorite spectator sports. I especially love going to a Dallas Stars game with Carson and asking him endless questions. He tolerates my ignorance quite well.

Little did we know Carson would someday be used by God to start a collegiate hockey program after his playing career. That wasn't some goal we made for our hockey-playing son when he first started playing the game at age six. It wasn't even on the radar! We never dreamed of God using him in that way. However, God knew. He was doing the work of planting the seeds there—writing that story on his heart, even at a young age. But, by God's grace, even though we couldn't see the end in mind, we had shared goals from the start. That made everything click.

We knew our why, and that made all the difference.

For any parent, that's the coolest thing on earth. Knowing God uses us, as parents, to help grow our children. What if we could continually remember that our children are God's children. Many days, our only objective should be to try and stay out of His way! There was a purpose behind the decision of Carson to fall in love with a sport so far afield from what we were used to. We were blessed with the opportunity to watch God take Carson and create an opportunity for him to build a lasting legacy that would touch hundreds of young men's lives.

The point to all this: you may not always know the end result that God has in mind for your children; but you *can know* your why. From the start. Get your why right and then watch how things fall into place.

To put this another way, some parents *just know* their child is destined to be the next Tom Brady. So, they force their child to try and fall in love with football. However, this same child might want to take another path. We need to let God sort that stuff out, and not predetermine or force the outcome.

Defining the purpose of youth athletics for your family is one of the most important aspects when your children head into the game. What does your family want from the game? How do you model this choice with your children? How can you support them, but not overwhelm them? What skills can they learn from the game? Why are we playing this game anyway?

Most of us might say that our children play the game because they enjoy it. It brings pleasure to our children and we get to have fun as a family. The exercise doesn't hurt either, especially as it can help balance out the other tech-saturated options for children.

Your response may also be influenced by where your family sits on the "competitiveness" spectrum. But, even the most intensely competitive family should have some understanding and shared goals around the purpose behind those long hours. We should enjoy the game and if we are spectators of our children, we should enjoy watching them compete. But, is that what's happening in youth sports today?

If pleasure, fun, excitement, and enjoyment are not happening in the state of youth sports, then what's wrong? Just maybe, the parents and coaches have hijacked the true purpose. We've made the game about us. And, when that becomes our purpose, the outcomes we seek get skewed.

I've seen two approaches parents often take with youth sports. First, some use it as training for a potential professional career or collegiate scholarship. Second, some use it as a place to do life and have their children learn valuable lessons. I'd strongly urge you to be in that second group.

Here's a fun exercise. Find a seven-year-old boy and ask him if he likes to play a sport and ask him which one is his favorite. Then, ask him *why he plays* that game. Listen closely to his answer.

Most likely, you'll hear something like, "Because, it's FUN!" Now, ask the same questions to a 14-year-old boy. Would it surprise you to know how much those answers change in just a few short years? The answers will be extremely varied, ranging from "fun" to "because my parents force me" to "because it's my dream to play professionally" to "because my friends play" or "just to stay busy."

So, are we missing the point? And, if we are, as parents and coaches, what can we do about it? How can we avoid the mistakes of having the wrong perspective, setting the wrong goals, and defining the wrong purpose in sports?

Let's settle the why question before moving forward. If that question isn't settled for your family, you're probably under more stress than you need to be. And, sadly, our children will suffer through their youth sports experience—and may get damaged on the other side.

So, what's the goal for your family when heading to sign ups for volleyball, soccer, baseball, or golf? I propose that in some form or another, you include development of your child's character as a primary goal for sports involvement. If your goal is not your child's character, then you may need to take a pause and reevaluate what this decision means for your family.

Ask yourself two very probing questions. First, "Is my child's participation in athletics about me and my desires?" And, second, "Am I encouraging them to play just so they get a scholarship or a pro contract?" If the answer to either question is "Yes," then I urge you to consider revisiting that before sign-ups for the next season get underway.

Far too many of us adults forget to ask these questions. If we apply ridiculous amounts of pressure to our children before they walk out on the field, why are we shocked when they have ridiculous attitudes when they walk off?

If our goal is our child's character growth, then we need to get out of God's way. Our children are gifts from God, and He has a plan for each of them. We don't get to *design* God's plan for our children, but we do get to *discover* it.

Almighty God has more control over their lives than we do! "But the plans of the LORD stand firm forever, the purposes of his heart through all generations" (Psalm 33:11, NIV). The plans God has for our children are way better than any plans we could ever dream up. Would it not be better for us to help our children discover God's plans for their lives than to fight for our own?

Here's my goal for us: I want us parents and coaches of girls, boys, women, and men in sports to be the best role models possible for our children. Ephesians 5:1 calls us to "Follow God's example, therefore, as dearly loved children." (NIV) God invites us to grow up by modeling our lives after Him. If we want to be the best for our children, then I see that invitation as a win-win. How can we fail, if we choose God as our model?

My prayer is this: "Lord, help us lead our families in Your ways, as we try to prepare our children. Help me, as a parent, to help and not hurt my children, especially as it relates to their playing games and learning about life and their faith. May I never be a hindrance to my children or to those I coach. Amen."

The fields truly are ripe for harvest. How you handle your why matters greatly. The opportunity to help our children live lives of character, influence, and joy is right in our hands. We can use youth sports to do this, but only if we share common goals. We can teach our children that success isn't about wins, and failure's not about losses. All this combines to give us a platform for character growth like no other. When we leverage it well, we honor God both as parents and as players of the game.

DIG DEEPER

1. What is your "why" for involving your children in sports?
2. What would your children say is their "why" for playing sports?
3. Would you say that each member of your family is aligned and aware of the reasons for playing sports? If the alignment's not quite there, what could you do to get everyone on the same page?
4. Can you say you're "following God's example" as it relates to having your child in sports? Why or why not?
5. How are your family's current athletic endeavors pointing your children toward God?

2 The Game Belongs to the Children

I t's Saturday morning in America.

The sports fields and gymnasiums are packed with children of all ages dressed in a colorful array of uniforms, armed with some of the greatest equipment ever designed, competing for the most beautiful plastic trophies. You know the scene. Parents, extended family, and friends all shouting encouragement and affirmation for their favorite players. Volunteer coaches, referees, and game officials joyfully making their presence known—and perhaps without even realizing it—investing in the future of America. The children.

You've seen it. Communities coming together and providing state-of-the-art facilities for children to play in and dream in. The local sports store owner celebrating as families fill his shop trying on the newest equipment and uniforms. City officials basking in the glory of the acres of land they smartly converted to be occupied by their fellow sports-minded families. The barber shop overflowing with locals swapping stories from the previous Friday night game that captured the town's attention. Local police enjoying a break from crime—knowing teens are burning all that energy on the courts instead of roaming the streets.

Is this an accurate picture of your neighborhood? Or, is this a day long gone in American youth sports? What has youth sports become and where is it going? More importantly, how can we, as parents of athletes, navigate this increasingly complex environment and keep the best interests of our children squarely in view?

This probably reads like a dream. It may be. Yet, is it possible— even probable—that we can reclaim sports to help us plant great seeds in the lives of our children and nurture them until the great harvest day? I think it is possible. I think it used to be that way. We can make it that way again. To get there, we must first figure out what went wrong. I believe the clues to this mystery are found when we look in the mirror. We have stolen something from our children.

As you read the description of Sports Mayberry above, could you see yourself in that picture? Are you one of those who contribute to the community of encouragement? Maybe you are a willing helper in your community sports environment who realizes that the game belongs to the children. Or, perhaps not. Maybe you're one of the untold numbers of parents across this country who have hijacked the sports experience and used it for their own enjoyment. You are one more member of the raving mob routinely yelling at the coach, "Put Johnny in!" Since, clearly, no one else's child compares to your little Johnny.

Today, about 40 million children under the age of 18 will play some form of organized sports. Alarmingly, according to a poll by the National Alliance for Youth Sports, more than 70 percent of them will drop out by the age of 13.* Why is this happening? And, what can we do about it? Should we even try to do anything about it?

I remember when my dream began. I was a 7-year-old sitting at my grandparents' kitchen table in Houston with my Uncle Chet. He was a baseball card collector and avid sports fan. I told Uncle Chet, "One day I'll have my own baseball card—with my face on it!" I don't remember his response. But, I determined then and there I would one day play in the Big Leagues.

I did not get there just because I was talented or worked hard. God's hand of blessing allowed me to fulfill my dream of playing professional baseball. The odds are against any young athlete who seeks to play at even the college level, much less professionally. Getting to the top may start with the dream, but it's God who sustains and gives the continual grace to continue in this pursuit. It takes commitment, dedication, perseverance, and mental toughness to live this dream—all of which ultimately comes from God.

I don't want to discourage your child from trying to fulfill his or her dream. If anything, I hope you and your child will dream bigger than you do now. I hope you become authors of your own accomplishment story. I encouraged my own sons to dream big, get after it, while understanding their ultimate purpose and mission in life, and that is to honor God in every way!

The question comes down to this: who is writing their stories? Are we, as parents, trying to carve that path for them? Or, are we

---

*Julianna W. Miner, *The Washington Post*. "Why 70 percent of kids quit sports by age 13". June 1, 2016. *https://www.washingtonpost.com/news/parenting/wp/2016/06/01/why-70-percent-of-kids-quit-sports-by-age-13/*

encouraging them to develop their talents, work hard, and dedicate themselves to figuring out where their dreams will lead? Where does God's plan for their life figure into all this?

This is the challenge of parenting young athletes. And, this opportunity to learn, strive, and dream can be fully explored within athletic endeavors. It's a God-given character development greenhouse where our children can grow in a safe, warm and well-fertilized environment. If we remember whose greenhouse it is.

I had big dreams for my three sons to play professional sports when they were young. My wife Christina and I determined that when our boys started playing sports, our job as parents was to encourage them. We should push them to have fun and be the best they could be at whatever sport they played. Above all, we taught our boys to leverage sports as a platform for other important endeavors like education, relationship building, and gaining life skills that transcend what happens on the playing field.

Over the years, however, I had to repeatedly remind myself: it's only a game. It's only a game. This is not life and death.

If you make your living by the game—then it's understandable for you to see it through a different lens. It's vital to your economic interests. But, are those economic interests life and death? Really? Why has the game become so important to us? Especially, in the context of youth sports, when none of those ten-year-olds out on those fields should be worrying about their next contract extension.

I've heard many times from the mouths of parents, "Making it to the next level is what matters. That's why the game is so important. And, it's my job to ensure they get there." If we understand our role as parents—as character-producing-parent-farmers—we'll be about the business of constantly looking for favorable conditions to yield the right crop. If our goal as farmers is to grown corn, then we plant corn. If we want wheat, we'd better plant some wheat. Many parents are planting the wrong seeds because they're chasing the wrong harvest.

The odd thing is that the bad seeds we're planting often look like good seeds. I regularly hear these kinds of "why's" from well-meaning parents:

- ". . . because my daughter will get a full ride to play basketball at her favorite Division-1 school . . ."
- ". . . because my daughter will be the next Olympic swimmer. . ."
- ". . . because my son will be the next Tiger Woods. . ."

That's an interesting word, "Because." What we want them to *be* becomes our *cause*. Be-cause.

However, I don't want to say that these goals are all bad. I'd just say they fall short on some level. They don't necessarily have the end in mind. I mean, you do recognize that even if your child becomes the next Hall of Famer, that he or she could live some 40 or 50 years beyond their playing days, right? Hopefully, you see their sports careers are a "fun middle" season (even if they "go pro") and don't represent the "end" of their life—either literally or figuratively.

If we have these shortsighted goals for our children, we have to also ask ourselves if those kinds of goals really have *the children* in mind?

What I also see are some underlying beliefs that parents have. These are like seeds we're planting too, only they are ones we don't really say out loud! We carry these seeds around with us, but we need to recognize that they're there through our actions. We think the game is so important, if we're honest:

- "... because as a parent, my personal pride rests on every goal, point, and touchdown my child scores ..."
- "... because my child will make enough money playing pro sports that he'll be able to rescue his family from this ordinary life ..."
- "... because I will gain more respect. I'll get bragging rights. I'll be able to puff my chest out on every street corner ..."

That's right, in many cases, the game is more important than life because it's all about us!

Tough questions, right? You bet they are. But, in this age of self-importance, self-focus, and self-centeredness, those questions must be answered. Honestly and ruthlessly.

We must always keep this in mind: the game belongs to the children.

When this gets kicked aside, the game turns into something it was not designed to become. We miss the point and miss our role as parent-farmers and coaches.

Truth be told, I loved baseball so much I would have played for free (funny, I never mentioned that to the Phillies or Brewers). Baseball was and still is a great passion for me and it provided more to me and my family than I could ever repay. I respect the game for what it is, and over time, for what it isn't. It's not a guaranteed ticket to riches and fame.

Even so, the longer I've lived and experienced the game with my family, friends, and as a coach of other children, I have realized something. Viewing myself as a farmer is a great way to see my role in youth sports. What seeds are we planting? What crop do we want to harvest? What are we cultivating?

The game provides an opportunity for us and our children. It is the escape from the daily grind and the opportunity to be with future generations. To enjoy life in many diverse ways. The game teaches us lessons that are hard to learn in other places. The game is beautiful and purposeful. It can bring us joy, rally us, and inspire us. The game drives us to pull together. The game helps us realize the playing field is level no matter what. The game shows us hard work pays off. The game teaches us how to power through adversity, overcome fear, and rise above chaos. The game also links generations, makes us laugh, cry, scream, curse, and celebrate.

Still, who does the youth sports game *belong* to?

That is the question every stakeholder involved needs to answer. I believe the game belongs to the children. That's how we respect it. The right and proper perspective is what needs to be taught, measured, and brought to account.

When fans and parents insert themselves into the game inappropriately, what happens? We've all been there. If you've been involved in sports, you've seen it. Parents and fans will steal the joy and interrupt the pureness and purpose of the game.

The training and development involved within youth sports is at an unprecedented level. We even see some overuse injuries that can occur with such deep and involved coaching and training sessions. When an 8-year-old baseball player has his own personal hitting, pitching, and defensive instructor—along with personal lessons three to five times per week—yet, he doesn't seem to have a passion for it, I wonder. Who wants to play more, the child or the parent?

I live in Southlake, Texas. Here, personalized coaching is quite common. Look around in most cities today. You'll find indoor baseball, volleyball, basketball, and multi-sports arenas dotting the landscape. There's a reason we don't see children playing in the streets anymore. They're all playing in custom-built gyms, parks, rec centers and campuses.

We've shifted from our roles as parent-farmers. We've become the people looking to punch a lottery ticket if Little Timmy shows promise as a future star. We've become a people who are too busy taking lessons and carting off to the weekend tournaments. If we like a sport, we assume that we must join a select league, take out a second mortgage and make a life out of it!

No doubt, the game has changed. So, as parents, what are we to do? How should we walk this whole sports thing out with our children so we can be a blessing and not a curse? How can we know what seeds we should plant and when?

There are a lot of great reasons to play a sport—especially as a child. But, let me be clear—those reasons need to have a Godward and character development aim. Anything besides that runs the risk of being counterproductive. Within this overall perspective, there are dozens of positive outcomes we see from youth sports. There are great secondary benefits from becoming involved.

In thinking about this, I sat down with my family and we quickly came up with no less than 50 reasons to get children involved in athletics. You won't find "get a scholarship" or "snag a gold medal" on the list that follows. There are many more reasons, but just for fun, let's walk through our family's list. Maybe our list will help inspire you and your family to build your own!

Physical Benefits:

1. Motor skills development
2. Cardiovascular fitness
3. Weight control
4. Physical strength
5. Muscular endurance
6. Emotional development
7. Behavioral development
8. Bone development & structure

Positive Social Outcomes:

9. Keeps children busy
10. Less time to get in trouble
11. Citizenship
12. Learn the power of teamwork
13. Learn how to respect others
14. Learn how to support others
15. Learn selflessness on a team
16. Learn the importance of roles
17. Learn the value of diversity
18. Learn communication skills
19. Learn rule following

Character Development:

20. Leadership skills taught and modeled
21. Learn how to be passionate
22. Learn how to be responsible
23. Learn time management
24. Learn how to win with humility
25. Learn how to lose with grace
26. Learn that God's love is not based upon performance
27. Learn how to overcome adversity and failure
28. Learn how to handle pressure
29. Learn patience
30. Learn the power of encouragement
31. Learn how to receive coaching
32. Learn how to give feedback
33. Learn the benefits of hard work
34. Learn a sense of initiative
35. See how discipline pays dividends
36. Learn how to control attitudes
37. Learn how others want to be treated
38. Learn the most talented don't always win
39. Learn how strong relationships & trust lead to better teamwork
40. Learn how to strategize
41. Learn how to make adjustments
42. Learn how to think on the fly
43. Learn that success breeds confidence
44. Learn how to compete
45. Learning how the influence of a good coach can make a difference
46. Learn how to work well with a team

47. Learn how to reach a common goal with a team
48. Learn how to have fun
49. Experience the joy of rewards
50. Learn that scoreboards are a meritocracy (the score is earned, not given)

There are also a number of reasons not to get your children involved in youth sports. After forty-five years of involvement, I've seen numerous improvements in how the game is used by parents, coaches and institutions. However, a great number of things have changed for the worse as well.

It seems youth sports get misused and twisted in two ways. On one hand, parents don't use youth sports correctly—as a tool for character development. On the other, I see coaches and institutions hijack youth sports for their own selfish gain. The result is that we now have a far different culture in youth sports than we had a generation ago. Following are a few reasons to be cautious or even not to let athletics into your children's lives.

Here are some reasons not to get your children involved in sports:

1. Protect them from adults who are different than you are
2. Protect them from losing confidence
3. Shield them from receiving criticism
4. Protect them from violence or aggression
5. Avoid damaging their self-esteem
6. Costs too much
7. Takes too much time

8.   Afraid child will get hurt
9.   Child is not athletic
10.   Child is too timid
11.   Can't get the child off video games (don't get me started . . .)
12.   Child is too lazy
13.   Child doesn't have a passion for sports
14.   There are no leagues for us to join

Take time to review this list. Overall, we often over-protect our children and we believe that if we just keep them from any discomfort, we're doing them a favor. We're not helping our children when we have them avoid all forms of struggle. Some appropriate challenge, pain, and resistance is actually necessary for the building of godly character.

We need to understand why our children are playing the game and make sure it's not about us. If we're pulling our children in selfish or prideful directions, we shouldn't be shocked when we have reaped what we've sown. If we keep this in mind, we can help them enjoy the freedom of "just playing" the game and seeing where it leads.

The game must belong to the children, and if we are wise stewards, we'll see it produce the results we want. Parents and coaches need these "reasons for" and "reasons against" lists in their minds. Such a list will provide clarity on how we can keep the game in the right hands. This allows the game to shape our children with godly character.

As a parent-farmer remember: You're the one with this list. You're planning the farm. You're the one planting the seeds. You're doing the weeding and cultivating. You're running the operation, so the crops are "free to grow" within the confines of a well-structured environment.

We can easily grow the wrong crop if we're not careful. Farms don't build and plant themselves. There's a farmer who's orchestrating what goes into that farm. If we believe this game is for us, we're planting bad seeds. Let's make sure the game belongs to the children. And, in doing this, we'll see that, ultimately, they will benefit greatly from the oversight of the master farmer. Because, in the end, everything belongs to God. We are only stewards.

DIG DEEPER

1. Review the list of "50 Reasons Why." What are your strongest "why's"?
2. What does the game mean to you?
3. How do we keep the game in perspective?
4. How do we prevent trying to live our lives through our children in sports?
5. Do you treat your actions and lessons related to sports as belonging to God? Explain.

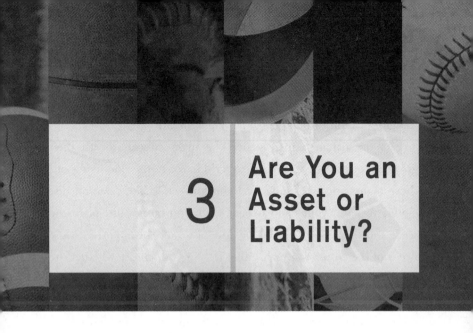

3 | Are You an Asset or Liability?

There is no such thing as the perfect parent.

If you're a young parent, you may still be trying to fight it. You believe you'll be the flawless parent, the one, the only. Best of luck on that. If you believe you're the only one who will make all the right decisions, never get upset, and by your amazing perfection, create the perfect child—I'm afraid you're in for a reality check.

I know you're probably not this deluded. At least, I hope not. You realize that neither you nor I will be the model of parental perfection. If that's true, then what should we strive for? What should be the standard we measure ourselves against? What's our goal? If perfection isn't attainable, what is?

One way to discern a reasonable answer to this question is to ask ourselves this: "As it relates to my children becoming all God intends for them to be, am I an asset or a liability?" In general, are we spurring them on toward love and good deeds, or are we getting in the way of their growth and development? Are we pointing them to God through their daily experiences, or are we feeding their appetite for self-glorification through personal achievement?

As the parent-farmer, you're the main contributor to their growth. You're in that day-to-day grind. You're the one living out those nights and weekends, and you know it'll take care and discipline to point your child toward God. You cannot just plant the seeds and then leave them alone. You also must be attentive to the needs of the crops. You realize that it's not your choice whether the sun rises or the rain falls. There are limits to your influence. However, you also don't want to step on a tender shoot and kill it before the roots take hold in the soil. You want to be intentional and purposeful but also recognize your limits along the way.

Even though we are limited, we aim to do everything possible to bring forth a strong harvest in the hearts and lives of our children. To possibly stretch the analogy to its limits, different crops often require unique approaches to nurture them into full health. The good parent-farmer understands that some crops require open space, while others need a trellis nearby to latch onto. There's not a one-size-fits-all approach to parent-farming. We constantly try to maximize the good we're doing, while minimizing the bad.

We may not be able to force a specific path for our children, but we strive to give them the right environment to spur growth and reduce unnecessary risk. We seek to give them every chance to become strong and fruitful.

As they grow, we sometimes prune the branches to keep them healthy. We add in the appropriate measure of discipline to ensure positive correction. This is highlighted in the book of Hebrews:

Endure hardship as discipline; God is treating you as his children. For what children are not disciplined by their father? If you are not disciplined—and everyone undergoes discipline— then you are not legitimate, not true sons and daughters at all. Moreover, we have all had human fathers who disciplined us and we respected them for it. How much more should we submit to the father of spirits and live! They disciplined us for a little while as they thought best, but God disciplines us for our good, in order that we may share in his holiness. No discipline seems pleasant at the time, but painful. Later on, however, it produces a harvest of righteousness and peace for those who have been trained by it. (Hebrews 12:7-11, NIV)

Finding this balance can be difficult. Do all the good you can, avoid the bad, give the right amount of discipline, but don't crush them. Finally, leave room for God to do what only he can do. This is an ongoing challenge for us parents.

This is difficult all by itself, but some of us make it even harder. We do this by trying to re-live our own lives through those of our children. We might not ever say it out loud. This sounds crazy, "Yes, I'm trying to realize all my lifelong dreams through my children."

Yet, some of us give in to this temptation more frequently than we'd care to admit. Before you dismiss this out of hand, think about it. Wouldn't you agree, that if you're chasing your own dreams through the life of your son or daughter, it's almost impossible to realize that you're doing it? This might be a blind spot for you. By definition, blind spots are hard for us to see all by ourselves. It can be hard to recognize that you are *that* parent. What we often need is a bit of outside help to see this for what it really is. You may gain perspective here by simply seeking input from someone like your spouse, your older children, or another parent who knows you well. We need truth-tellers around us. It's essential.

If none of those people are with you right now, let's begin with at least an attempt at personal introspection to get the ball rolling. Consider whether you're one of my two least favorite kinds of parents: the helicopter parent or the lawnmower parent.

How can you know if you're the helicopter parent? Well, there's a fine line. But, consider whether you take an excessive interest in your children by trying too hard to carve their path for them. I'm no child (or adult) psychologist, but I've observed the effects of over-parenting. It's an unhealthy epidemic. I see many parents attempt to show God (and the world) how they're in charge of navigating the course of our children's lives. This excessive interest plays out in multiple ways.

The helicopter parent hovers over their children's every move. You may be this person if you constantly oversee every aspect of your child's sports life. For example, if you *must* coach your child's team, even though you have zero experience in that particular sport, then you might be *that* parent. Or, if you find yourself propping up your child after a poor performance, in order to save their self-confidence, then you might be that parent. (There's a reason it's called "self-confidence"). If you're telling your son or daughter the coach is crazy and they deserve more playing time, there is a real good chance that you deserve the label. Finally, if you have become your child's self-appointed college recruiting coordinator, you are definitely that parent.

Or, maybe you're the lawnmower parent. You believe your role in life is to be the great obstacle remover. You want to mow down all of your child's challenges, struggles, or discomforts in life. You want to ensure she has no hurdles to clear on her way to athletic glory. Sadly, your children will be easy for others to spot. They'll be the ones who aren't ready to persevere through difficult times. They will be the ones who give up too easily and complain too quickly. They will not have developed the necessary resilience to push through challenges.

The lawnmower parent often resorts to various types of nuanced and manipulative behaviors. Some of them come to all the games with a notepad or app on their phone so they can track everyone's playing time. Then, they chase down the coaches to discuss the insights they've found in these stats. They couch this feedback as a favor to the coach, when in reality they're simply trying to illustrate the imbalance of the sports universe evidenced by their child's insufficient time in the game.

Some of them volunteer to help, or even invite the coach over for dinner, all in an effort to ensure the coach looks more favorably on their child. Most coaches can easily spot the motive behind these moves, so don't think you're kidding anyone if this is your approach.

These relatively mild lawnmower parent shenanigans often escalate as the stakes get higher. The same parents who try to curry favor from a high school coach are the ones who end up actually bribing a college coach to give their child a good look. The tactics move from counterproductive and irritating to immoral and illegal.

The challenge for us parents is to be just the right amount of helpful. If we overhelp, we hamstring our children's sports careers, and in many cases, their approach to life overall. The children of the helicopter and lawnmower parents simply don't make it far in athletics. They haven't built the capacity to overcome adversity and learn from defeat, which are two of the essential ingredients for athletic (and life) success.

Of course, there are various imbalanced ways of parenting in sports. These are just a couple that I've seen over and over. Some children have parents who berate them on the field, or who never come to games at all. There are difficult circumstances that children haven't really signed up for, but they must learn to endure and survive through them, difficult as it can be to watch.

If you resemble any of these parenting personas, do your child a favor and cut it out! Covering for your children's mistakes, catching their every fall, or trying to carve a painless path will set them up for failure later in life. When we find ourselves getting upset with our children over athletic outcomes, we need to get a grip. We all know, nobody ever played the game better than we did. Eh-hem. We must refrain from killing our children's spirit with our behavior. It will only serve to diminish their will to succeed.

I'll never forget Joey, the young man I met while on a business trip to Cincinnati several years ago. He and one of his childhood friends were talking about their younger days in baseball. We quickly connected the dots. We had competed against each other in a Palomino World Series event when we were 16 years old!

When he mentioned his name, I told him I remembered exactly who he was. He was a right-handed pitcher who threw absolute gas (read: he threw a baseball very hard)! He'd been projected as an MLB draft pick after his Senior year of high school. I asked him about his career, which I hadn't remembered, and his buddy stepped in to explain. He told me Joey's Dad was a tyrant and made life very difficult for him. He would routinely berate Joey if he made the slightest mistake with comments like, "You are an embarrassment to me and our family. You should quit ball. You're a joke."

So, what did Joey do with that promising baseball career? He quit the game. He showed his Dad, alright. He decided one day that he'd had enough. He would no longer allow his brutal father to define him as a young man by how he played the game.

Joey's story is, unfortunately, not that unusual. We all make mistakes. I am not the perfect parent. Christina has made one or two herself. As far as I know, there is no parents Hall-of-Fame where all the flawless moms and dads are enshrined as examples for us to ooh and aah over. I've made plenty of mistakes, and most of the time they were tied to an injustice committed, usually by a terrible umpire. I have yelled and acted like a total knucklehead on more than a few occasions.

Long ago I gave my wife and sons full permission to call me out if they thought I crossed the line. I have received a number of elbows in the ribs from my beautiful, yet tough, bride, for making derogatory comments about umpires. Yes, I am a sinner! I have also apologized and asked forgiveness many times. When my behavior becomes an embarrassment to my children, that's a problem. I was thankful my family would call me to account when those instances occurred. We all need accountability and perspective from people who love us. These are people who care enough about us not to allow us to stay the way we are. They step in when we need correction.

There's an interesting truth about competitive athletics: the scoreboard is a meritocracy. It doesn't care if the points were put up by a rich kid or a poor kid, a black one or white one, or one that has helpful parents or destructive parents. It only rewards the effectiveness on the field.

In that sense, the playing field is level when you let go of little Johnny's hand and he crosses those white lines. Your disservice as an overly controlling parent will land your child directly on the bench, and that's only if he or she makes the team. Your child won't last in athletic competition. Only the strong will survive, as they climb to higher levels of competition. And we only get strong by overcoming resistance.

Let's be careful not to protect our children so much that we cripple them. Not all crops need to grow indoors. Some die that way. Corn only grows out in the sun! Well, unless it's some weird bioengineered variety, and who wants that?

My point: we can overprotect our children, but at what cost?

Finally, some quick checks to see if you're the overprotective parent type. Have you ever endorsed the acceptance of participation trophies? I realize there may be some disagreement about getting a trophy for showing up. I firmly believe kids learn nothing from a trophy they receive just for being present. That trophy may even cause more harm than good down the road.

Have you ever been involved in a "fun, fair, positive" league (which means, "we don't keep score")? If you think 4 and 5-year-olds don't keep score, I have news for you. Or worse, do your children play in a league where they limit the good players from scoring points beyond some "fair" arbitrary standard. What about the more subtle coddling of your young athlete, constantly telling them how talented or gifted he or she is? Have you ever been untruthful regarding their poor performance? Or, what about constantly defending your children's poor attitude to coaches, officials, and other players?

As I mentioned before, if you ask any parent whether they fit one of these labels, most likely, they will not admit it. Actually, they *cannot* admit it. They simply don't realize they're falling into these destructive patterns. This is where the power of feedback comes into play. How do we know we're parenting appropriately? We need honest friends and family to step up, be bold and courageous, and tell us. If they are not telling us, we need to ask.

One of my great mentors is Flip Flippen. I know, great name (yes, that's his real name). An even greater man. I've had the pleasure of working with him for many years and he helped me break a critical personal constraint in this area. It didn't take Flip long to realize I was one of those guys who overplayed my strength of being overly nurturing.

My strong desire to connect, encourage, and please people could sometimes become a liability. I didn't want people to walk away feeling bad after an interaction. I wanted everybody who knew me to love me. Taken to the extreme, this behavior is a huge constraint and gets in the way of coaching, teaching, and helping others develop. This affected my own children. Through Flip's coaching, I was able to break through this personal barrier and become a much better disciplinarian as a father.

I was one of those men who could not wait to have children. I look at each of my sons and thank God every day for the privilege of becoming a father. Early in their lives my wife was a stricter disciplinarian. It was a wake-up call for me to realize that I needed to step up and not rely on my wife to discipline our sons when they needed correction. It would pain me to do it, but looking back, I am so thankful that Flip and others helped me to strengthen those parenting skills. My sons were the greatest beneficiaries of my newly found ability to step in when needed. I had broken through a constraint!

Personal growth is not just personal. We need truth-tellers to step in and provide the hard, honest feedback—if we want to grow. If we don't get it, those unacknowledged constraints can bite us and affect the people around us. If we want to be the best parents to our children and young athletes, we need to know if we are hindering them or empowering them. If you are coddling your children in an unhealthy way, the end product will not be a desirable one.

Let's get this right. Just as a farmer can over-water or under-water his crop, we parent-farmers must learn to assess ourselves and ask people around us to discover whether we're being an asset or a liability.

I believe the story of young Tiger Woods can help us see how parents can be both an asset and a liability. Even unintentionally so. You may recall Tiger's father, Earl Woods, was a major influence in Tiger's life. I may never forget when Tiger made his "professional" debut one night on the Mike Douglas show in 1978.

Tiger was a young golfing protégé, who was projected toward greatness, even at the tender age of 2 years old. Earl Woods, by most measures, was a powerful force and good man in Tiger's life. Could there have been some helicopter or lawnmower parenting going on? That's hard to measure, and I wasn't there. The stories we did hear over time seemed to indicate that Tiger had a disciplined and prioritized schedule when it came to golf. Earl seemed to be preparing him for a life as a professional golfer. And, as it related to success on the golf course, the numbers would indicate that Earl's planning and Tiger's hard work paid off.

However, did either of those men get precisely what they wanted, in the long haul?

The questions for us as parents of young athletes is this: what are we doing that will make a long-term difference in the character of our children? And, what happens when we're no longer in their day-to-day lives to walk alongside and correct their problems? Are we building lives for the future or getting in the way of their development? Are we preparing our children for the path or are we getting in the way of them learning how to cope with failure? Earl was doing his best to prep Tiger for the PGA Tour, and based on what I can see, he did his level best to achieve that.

Even so, as parents who are trying to honor God, our goals should include life after sports and even a God-honoring life during sports.

I don't know if you've caught this yet, but my passion is still the game of baseball. My Little League "career" was the foundation of this passion. I had the great blessing of being coached by incredible men. In youth ball, Fred Burns, a former Little League World Series champion from Houston, was my coach for several years. His son Ed is a dear friend even to this day. Fred taught me (and many other children) the fundamentals of the game and also how to play the game with honor.

His greatest lesson for me didn't come on the baseball field. It came on the golf course. His family took me on vacations over several summers. When Ed and I were 13 years old, Fred took us to play golf at Galveston Country Club. On one of the greens, I became angry after missing a putt and threw my club. Fred walked over calmly and took my arm, looked me straight in the eye and said, "That's not how we behave on the golf course. Or, anywhere else for that matter." I'll never forget that moment.

Fred was a mild-mannered man. I only saw him get angry a couple of times throughout our long relationship. During an All-Star baseball game against a neighborhood rival, I got steamrolled. I was covering home plate as an opposing player came running from third base. I was a pretty big kid, but I got destroyed on that play. I found myself on the ground with sore ribs, a bloody lip and seeing stars.

The umpire didn't make the right call. He should've ejected the perp and called him out for the mandatory slide rule in Little League. When Fred questioned the call, the opposing coach came storming out of the dugout and got in Fred's space. Fred backed away and then I heard him raise his voice for the first time in my life. He defended me and then asked the umpire to get help from his crew. After a few minutes the umpiring crew correctly interpreted the rule and the opposing player was ejected. Even better, their coach got tossed as well! It was a glorious moment! Fred Burns got angry and I got to see it, for only the second time in my life.

Coach Fred was a huge help to me. A parent-farmer, even though he wasn't my parent. He cared about my character and how I handled my anger. He was looking for more from me than raw talent or skill. Sadly, throwing my golf club wasn't the only mistake I've made in life. I've made tons, and many of them involved my boys and my wife.

I'm thankful that my wife, my children, and fellow coaches supported me by holding me accountable. I've always known that my drive to win carried the risk of me getting too emotional. If you know me personally, I realize that's a major understatement and you're probably laughing as you're reading this! Yeah, yeah, go ahead.

But the good news is this: I have learned to ask for help in this area. I've asked for accountability and given permission to others in my life so they can tell me when I need to shut up or take it down a notch.

The parent-farmer recognizes the fields are ripe and the work is too important to leave to our whims and failures. We have the potential to teach and discipline our children. God has given us a great responsibility. Our hands hold great potential and our actions have consequences, for better or worse.

Before we turn over the dirt and start planting, we must know our why. As part of that purpose, we want to ensure that the children own the game. Then, when we have a good reason and we're sure that we're in this sports thing for the right reasons, we're well positioned. From that vantage point, we can clearly see how to be an asset instead of a liability. And, if we get blinded to that reality, there are those around us that we've recruited to kick us in the tail when needed.

Parents are farmers, and farmers should always be cultivating. We strive to strike the right balance between endangering the crop and being overprotective. Some sun and rain is not only a good thing, it's essential for growth to occur.

We can work, as parent-farmers, in the fields of youth sports to reap an amazing harvest. When we don't do this, our children suffer. When we do it, our children can thrive. But, it's even bigger than that. Getting this right isn't just about your child, but it's about future generations.

After all, these things aren't left to other parents or even to the coaches. This is our job. God will bring the growth, but He asks us to work the fields. We realize in all this that we can only control the portion we can control. At some point, all we can do is point our children to God, then we're depending on Him bringing the right ingredients to allow them to truly flourish.

In the next section, let's dig even deeper and talk about planting the right seed. Roll up your sleeves.

DIG DEEPER

1. What's your biggest goal as a parent—related to your child playing youth sports?
2. What's one thing you can do to become more of an asset to your child?
3. Are you more likely to be a helicopter or lawnmower parent? Why?
4. Do you have a truth-teller in your life? If not, how long will it take you to find one?
5. When you make a mistake, are you quick to seek forgiveness and move forward?

SECTION TWO

PLANTING THE RIGHT SEED

"So, every healthy tree bears good fruit, but the diseased tree bears bad fruit. A healthy tree cannot bear bad fruit, nor can a diseased tree bear good fruit. Every tree that does not bear good fruit is cut down and thrown into the fire. Thus, you will recognize them by their fruits."
Matthew 7:17-20

4 | Three Laws of Sowing and Reaping

You remember my friend Cal. My visit to his farm brought the biblical reference of sowing and reaping to life for me. It moved from a concept to a concrete visual. I'd like to help you see it clearly as well by joining me on a visit to his farm someday. That may not happen soon, so let's take a swipe at it here in this chapter.

There are three laws of sowing and reaping. Put simply, they play out like this:

*Law #1: You get **what** you plant. If you want corn, plant corn.*
*Law #2: You get it **later** than you plant it. Plant now, reap later.*
*Law #3: You get **more** than you plant. One seed might yield hundreds of kernels.*

One of the things Cal's farm produces are carrots. He's never surprised when the carrots come out of the ground. He knew what he was planting when he put the seed down. The seed corresponds to the vegetable he gets at the end of the season. This isn't brain surgery, and the correlation to raising godly children is blatant and crucial for us to understand.

However, I see a ton of parents operating as if they don't grasp this at all. They get this totally wrong. Then, they're befuddled when they don't get what they expected.

Matthew 7:17-18 says, "So, every healthy tree bears good fruit, but the diseased tree bears bad fruit. A healthy tree cannot bear bad fruit, nor can a diseased tree bear good fruit." I strive to honor God with my life. I practice spiritual disciplines like praying, attending church and other aspects of the Christian faith. I love reading the Bible. No book has been translated, copied, or read as much as the Bible. It contains comfort and care for every human problem we will ever face. It is also my blueprint for doing life. I believe it's my responsibility to teach my sons about God through His Word.

So, what does this have to with sowing and reaping? If we want to raise children of character, what should we model?

Christina and I are thankful for parents who modeled character for us. Christina's mom, Paula, was a lifelong educator. In fact, Mrs. Jacobson, back in the day, was my fourth-grade teacher. Christina and I didn't know each other or date until her senior year of high school, but we put it together when I walked into her home to meet her mom for the first time. Paula modeled what a hard-working, single mother had to do to provide for her family. She raised two incredible, family-oriented, strong women who have become incredible parents to six boys.

My parents, Dennis & Claudia, were married when I was eight years old. My biological parents divorced when I was 5 years old, and my Mom married Dennis, who quickly adopted my sister and me and raised us as his own. My mom is known throughout our community as a passionate and loving mom. Any of our children or their friends will tell you how loud and encouraging "MeMa" is in the stands. She's always been there for our children and is my greatest fan.

In fact, during my first game in Philadelphia for the Phillies in 1989, the headline in the *Philadelphia Daily Post* was, "Combs and Mom defeat Pirates in Debut." And, yes, that cost me dearly in our next "Kangaroo Court" meeting with my professional teammates! My dad, Dennis, stepped into my life at just the right moment and provided discipline that was desperately needed. My life would have turned out much differently had it not been for Dennis Combs.

Our parents planted the right seeds. We have tried to continue that trajectory and plant the right seeds with our sons. You may wonder, "What *are* the 'right' seeds?" I'm glad you asked.

Before we dive in and take a look at some of the good seeds we should be planting, let me share about a time when I planted the wrong ones.

My son's team was playing in a summer tournament in Flower Mound, TX. That part of Texas—well, any part of Texas—isn't exactly known for its mild summer temperatures. If I recall correctly, that particular day, we were seeing the thermometers hit 105-degrees. It was brutal. Unfortunately, my son had an overly competitive, irresponsible and abusive head coach (that would be yours truly).

As the day wore on, we kept winning, but our back-up catcher couldn't play due to injury. So, Casey caught the first two games. Depending on your point of view, we were fortunate enough to make it to the Championship game. Casey convinced me (it didn't take much) to let him catch that third game so he could "win it for his teammates." It was a foolish decision.

During the game, Casey started complaining of a terrible headache, a surefire sign that he was suffering from heat-related problems. One of the parents in the stands who didn't realize what was occurring gave him some Excedrin. Due to the caffeine in those pills, they speed up your heart rate, which is one of the worst things you can do for someone about to have a heat stroke. He collapsed on the bench. When he woke up several minutes later, he was in the back of an ambulance covered in ice packs.

Let's get a full-scale blame game going. First up, overcompetitive coach. Guilty. Next, a league that schedules three-game sets in the blazing Texas summer heat. Also guilty. Finally, there's the irresponsible and reckless father? Oh, right. I already mentioned him. I mean me.

The point here is that if we're trying to teach our kids that winning is more important than actually staying alive, great job. Success. But, when we do this routinely to children in sports, then, after being at it ten years, wonder why they cheat, steal and wildly chase victory at any cost, we need to see the correlation.

Let's get back on track here. What are those seeds that we *should* be planting?

I think they start and end with love. The model Jesus teaches us—and one we most honor as His followers—is to love unconditionally. Unconditional love is a great concept, but actually living it out can be quite a challenge.

I have made many mistakes. I'll continue to make them, I'm sure. I hope I'll make them less frequently and that they'll be less and less damaging. When I was younger, my parents guided me and helped me avoid some huge ones. The unconditional part of that love was enormous. We knew even as children that whenever we made mistakes, our family would receive us and accept us. Of course, we were accountable when we made mistakes. Yet, we always knew we were loved. There was never a doubt about that.

I think what helped me avoid the major mistakes were the seeds they planted earlier in my life. These were seeds of honor, integrity, loyalty, and putting "family first." These and others had been firmly drilled into me at an early age. We planted those same seeds with our sons along the way. We added a few and put them into this priority: God first, family second, then serve and love our neighbors.

Getting the right seed in mind is the biggest piece of this puzzle. We must know what we want to reap so we can know what to plant. Then, the second law of sowing and reaping kicks in. We nurture those seeds to maturity over time. Sometimes, this is a waiting game and we need patience to see it through.

Cal showed me how law number two is brought to life on his farm. When he plants, they stagger the fields and turn them over often, in order to capture a greater yield. Certain vegetables grow better at certain times of the year, depending on a number of variables like weather and soil conditions. Carrots normally require three months from the time the seed hits the ground until they're gathered in. Potatoes and onions take even longer.

The application for parents is critical. There are times when we're planting seeds that can take years before they grow to full maturity. It can be a painstaking process. The variables that life throws at our children can be dangerous, like a late-Spring frost just after planting.

Or, they can even be a devastating flood that takes out a crop just before it ripens. Not long ago, Cal experienced a major weather challenge that cost their farm millions of dollars in lost crops.

We may plant incredible seed, nurture it diligently, and then still see the dreams, hopes, and plans for our teenagers vanish with one bad decision or unfortunate event.

We've walked alongside dozens of parents who have experienced incredibly painful moments when their children made poor choices or simply got caught up in the wrong crowd at the wrong time. Count us in on participating in some of those questionable moments with our boys. We have also witnessed many glorious moments with our sons and their friends when those seeds grew to produce incredible outcomes. I've had the joy of watching many of the boys and young men I've coached blossom into great athletes, students, and honorable citizens.

Despite the challenges that life can throw at us, I think the key has always been to know what we're planting and then just stay consistent. We sometimes just need to keep planting good seed and then react as well as we can when life's storms and pests come against our children.

Cal strives to give his crops the absolute best care after those seeds have been planted. He'll water appropriately, fertilize judiciously, and apply protective measures against the bugs and weather. Then, he waits patiently for the harvest. A ton of work, patience, perseverance, and prayer (then, more prayer) go into each season of planting. Just like life.

The last great lesson I learned from Cal's farm was when we took the short drive to the warehouse and distribution plant. This is where

I saw the final product being placed on conveyor belts. The vegetables were cleaned, closely inspected, parceled, bagged, and placed in crates for delivery.

Cal explained that when everything comes together on the farm just right, he always gets a lot more crop yield than seeds he planted. Of course, there are some years when the conditions simply don't allow for it. But Cal and his family have mastered the art of raising tremendous crops. They've developed strong expertise in the process. Now, they can't control every variable, but those they can control are controlled exceptionally well.

Isn't this just like God? When we follow His laws, plant great seeds, and nurture them in His ways, we can expect a tremendous harvest. As parent-farmers, we cannot control all the variables either. We can only control our effort in striving to do life right and with the right guidance. I know how hard it has been trying to raise three sons. I can't fathom how parents do it without God!

We live in a sin-sick world that is out to steal our children's souls. With our sons we've experienced the day-to-day battles with a world engulfed in pornography, drugs, alcohol, trying to fit in, addictive behaviors, video games and social media. It's a nonstop war.

When I read John 15, I come to understand that when we're attached to God's vine, we will reap more than we can imagine. The laws of sowing and reaping come alive, as God applies this metaphor to bearing much fruit. Verses four and five say this:

Abide in me, and I in you. As the branch cannot bear fruit by itself, unless it abides in the vine, neither can you, unless you abide in me. I am the vine; you are the branches. Whoever abides in me and I in him, he it is that bears much fruit, for apart from me you can do nothing. (John 15:4-5)

How do we bear much fruit for God? We walk with Him daily. There is no greater lesson for our children than teaching, mentoring, and modeling them to have daily interaction with a God who loves them and wants them to live abundant lives. The verses in John 15 also lead us to a deeper understanding of purpose, which is to love others. The application of John 15 will lead us to a more meaningful life and with every relationship God brings our way.

One of the greatest benefits of our boys playing baseball, football, hockey, and basketball were the incredible relationships we developed during those seasons. One of the coolest things about sport is this: it's one huge fraternity.

In baseball, I have come to know three generations of people who played, coached, organized, or were involved as a fan or supporter. Many of my closest friendships, mentors, and business relationships have involved incredible people I met through the game. The game hasn't defined my life, but the people associated with the game have been huge influences on me and my family.

This is the power of "who." I can honestly say I have never suffered a lonely moment in my life, because of my "who." These are the people I chose to surround myself with and they are continually involved in my life, and not just because I was in the game, but because of the relationships I was able to develop because of it.

Ed Burns and I grew up together, mostly at his house. Ed was my Sharpstown Little League teammate. I'm thankful his parents put up with me over those young teen summers. Ed and I reunited when we coached our own sons at Lamar Little League in Richmond, Texas. We laughed at the circle of life when Ed and Stephanie moved into the Richmond area with their three children.

During my son's playing days at Lamar, I had the privilege of coaching with people who would become some of my closest friends. Most of the families involved with our team became family to us and still are today. Amazingly, we still have a close group of "Dragon" parents from our Southlake athletics days. Our children all graduated years ago from Carroll High School, but we still get together for Dragon football and other social outings.

There are countless families I came to know through coaching and hundreds of friendships that developed from our time in Little League sports. Then, as our boys grew and hit the high school years, those teammates also became like family. Christina's home cooking brought many of those boys to our home over the years. The relationships we've built through athletics have been a key piece of our lives.

John 15:12 says, "This is my commandment, that you love one another as I have loved you." Then, verse 13 follows by saying, "Greater love has no one than this, that someone lay down his life for his friends." Relationships are crucial.

Youth sports will allow you and your family to connect with many people, and we need to ask ourselves, what's the point of all that? Many parents are planting seeds of character, integrity, hard work, discipline, and teamwork. Even so, there's a temptation in this world to plant seeds of competition at all costs, seeds of "winning is all that matters," seeds of "when we disagree, let's yell and fight it out." Through all of this, we must not forget the three laws of sowing and reaping. We reap what we sow. We reap it later than when we planted it. And, we reap more than we planted.

DIG DEEPER

1. What are the three laws of sowing & reaping?
2. How do these laws apply to your life as a coach or parent of athletes?
3. Read John 15. What might God be saying to you through this chapter—as it relates to your child and sports?
4. What's one thing you need to change—in seeking to apply John 15 to your life, as a parent?
5. What's your best memory as a child—either as a player or fan—related to sports? Tell that story to your child.

5 What Are You Planting?

The question we discussed earlier is worth revisiting: Why are we involving our children in youth sports at all?

If you're still wrestling with that question, it's okay. Most people struggle answering this question. When I was growing up, my why was incredibly self-centered. So, what changed for me? My life did a 180-degree flip when I came to understand Jesus Christ is who He said He is.

I didn't grow up in a religious home. The only time I heard God's name mentioned was when it was attached to a curse word. Don't get me wrong. I had a tremendous family. I couldn't have picked a more loving mom and dad. We just weren't into church or religious affiliations. My mom took us to church on the important holidays, but there wasn't a real connection to the Christian faith as a child.

That doesn't mean my life was a mess growing up. I simply didn't have a higher purpose or answer for my why other than playing ball, working hard in school, and living life on my own terms. I worked extremely hard. I was a straight "A" student. I excelled in baseball.

And, I partied hard with my buddies. I never really had a steady girlfriend in high school. I dated. But girls were more of an object to be conquered in my younger, more selfish, years. My mom and dad did their best to instill better values regarding other people, but I was a self-centered, self-absorbed young man until age 22. Then, my life changed. I met Jesus.

My focus from when I was a seven-year-old boy until I made it to professional baseball was to one day put on that big-league uniform. I graduated Summa Cum Laude from college. I was drafted in the first round of the 1988 MLB draft. I'd just finished playing on the 1988 US Olympic gold medal winning team. I had the most beautiful girlfriend in the world.

I was on top of the world.

I attended Major League Spring training camp in 1989 and put that Phillies uniform on for the first time. I can't describe the feeling when I looked in that mirror in the locker room to see those beautiful maroon pinstripes with the Phillies script across my chest. I had made it. This is what I had focused on for most of my waking moments. My feet didn't hit the ground for at least a week. And then, some feelings I can't fully describe began to take hold.

There was an empty feeling as I wondered, "This can't be all there is to it, can it?" I'd worked my entire young life to achieve this incredible goal that only a few people in the world ever get a chance to accomplish. Yet, there was this feeling that something was missing.

In Major League Baseball spring training, pitchers and catchers typically report about a week ahead of other players. This is because pitchers and catchers are the hardest working players in the game! (to my former teammates: you knew I was going to go there, didn't you?).

I was in the spring training camp of 1989 as a rookie player. The other position players arrived in late February. If you are a Phillies fan, you'll remember that this would end up being Mike Schmidt's final season as a Philadelphia Phillie.

Mike Schmidt was one of the greatest power-hitting third basemen to ever play the game. Mike was also an all-around great guy and team leader. When Mike walked into the clubhouse, it was like seeing a mini-god to this 22-year-old rookie. He was impressive and handled himself in the most professional manner.

So, on our first Sunday together in camp, Mike walks into the clubhouse and announces the team Chapel service would begin next door in the media room in 15 minutes. I didn't think much of it at first. I was required to go to chapel services at Baylor University. I attended one or two during my two years. This time was different, though. I mean, the future Hall-of-Famer just announced that Chapel was ready to begin.

I felt inclined to join but wasn't sure why. The reason became clear about five minutes into the service. Vince Nauss, the leader of Baseball Chapel, introduced a local Clearwater pastor named Steve Kreloff.

In his opening remarks, Steve declared he was raised in a Jewish home but had come to realize that Jesus was the Messiah. Jesus was the one prophesied about in the Old Testament. Now, that really flipped me out. I'd never heard of a Jewish guy becoming a Christian. I grew up in Texas, where Catholics were Catholic, Jews were Jewish, and most Texans were Baptist.

Steve's message that morning captured my full attention. After he spoke, he invited the room full of ballplayers to pray with him. In his prayer, he asked that if anyone had not yet trusted Jesus as their Savior to pray with him. For some reason, in that moment, it hit me: I had never asked Jesus to be my Savior.

Before Steve finished his prayer with our heads bowed, he asked for any hands to go up and I must have been the only one who raised my hand. Steve approached me as we were leaving the media room and he asked if I would be willing to meet with him to discuss my decision. We met a few days later and that became the start of a life-long friendship. Steve, and his son Ben, flew up for my MLB debut later that Summer and we've stayed in touch ever since that Spring day in 1989.

Think for a moment: who was your favorite coach, teacher, or mentor? What makes this person stand out in your mind? I'm willing to bet it was someone who had a profound impact on you in some way. They may have taught you an invaluable lesson, come alongside you at just the right moment, or intervened in a difficult situation. That relationship didn't just accidentally happen. There were seeds planted that made it possible for that mentor to impact your life.

My farmer friend, Cal, reminded me that planting season is the most important time for his farm. One would think it might be harvest season, but that's the fun part. Cutting down the grown crops and getting them ready for distribution is rewarding, because that means the crops are mature and they survived the challenges thrown at them.

But, planting. That's the most critical step. The conditions must be right and the soil ready. If the ground is too wet, that's a no-go. If the dirt is not conditioned appropriately, the seed will struggle. As the seed begins to grow, there must be the right amount of water and nutrition or the plant will not grow to its maximum potential.

I'm thankful for the people who came along in my life and made an investment in me. For some, they planted. Others watered. Of all these deep and lasting relationships that came through the game, I chose to become closest with those whose values of faith and family first aligned with mine. My playing days came and went in what seemed like a millisecond, but the relationships I made have lasted much longer.

This is one of the blessings of reaping what we sow. We sowed a lot of friendship seeds in sports over the years. And, ever since, we've been continually reaping those rewards.

Let's make an agreement right now, right here. We'll agree first that sports is an incredible platform for teaching our children some of the most important life skills they can learn. Second, let's also agree that many seeds can be planted. We get the opportunity to do much of the planting, but so do other coaches and teachers. Others will come along and water those seeds.

If our children are going to maximize their gifts and talents, our plan must include an intentional process of laying great seed, watering just the right amount, and helping them to navigate through the challenges. Then, once we've done the planting and watering, we must learn to manage instead of trying to control every moment. We need to allow other people and other forces to continually shape their growth.

We can't control their environment and as we've discussed already, we can't try to keep them from every failure. It's okay for our children to fail. Failure is a great teacher and motivator. Failing along the way is like the vine bumping into a rock. If it's going to survive and thrive, it'll need to find a way around that rock.

Your children learning how to fail and get back up is essential if they're going to succeed in any sport. They should learn how to fail forward. Let's fail like Logan Stout proclaims. He's one of my dear friends, and he's one of the best select baseball coaches in the country. He says, "Boys, if we are going to stink, let's stink fast." There's no time to get stuck in failure. Analyze, learn and move forward, quickly!

If we don't allow our children to suffer and feel the pain of losses or cuts from teams, they may never learn the valuable lessons athletes (and businesspeople and educators and preachers . . .) need in their toolboxes. Overcoming failure is a great self-propelling adventure. When we've worked through one, it makes us all the more ready to face others in the future. There is no doubt the reason some of our greatest leaders come from sports is that they learn how to grow through failure.

I had a great conversation with a Major League Scouting Director just prior to the most recent MLB Draft. I asked him to share the most critical factor he looks for in a baseball player today, beyond raw talent. He told me, "Without a doubt, I want to know how that kid handles adversity." He continued, "I see more high school players today cry and whine when things don't go their way. It's almost like they want someone to feel sorry for them or for their parents to intervene and save them from failure."

He put it like this, "I want that tough-minded, gritty, and get-after-it type of player, who when he strikes out, there's a look in his eye like, that is *not* going to happen again. He won't get me next time." He and I agreed that these kinds of players are getting harder and harder to find.

This is how I think we've gotten here, as a society. My experience with young players suggests that the self-esteem gobbledygook we have been feeding them for the past few decades has created a generation who doesn't know how to handle adversity and defeat. We have coddled them so much that they're ineffective and unprepared.

And, this is crucial if we're going to understand the sowing and reaping laws and how they play out in the lives of our children. If we sow the seed of avoiding small failures, we'll reap major fear. If we sow the seed of over-praising them, we'll find it produces pride and arrogance.

Does the name Bruce Matthews mean anything to you? Well, he's one of the all-time greatest offensive linemen in NFL history. He competed for 19 seasons. More remarkably, he played 293 consecutive games without missing due to injury. As a lineman. In the National Football league. Amazing.

He's part of the famed "Matthews" family of football players. Over the last five decades, there have been nine Matthews players who made it to the top level in this highly competitive sport. Nine players. Are you kidding me! Bruce is a Hall-of-Famer and he and his wife Carrie have been friends for twenty-five years. They've raised seven children, including three of those nine NFL'ers. And, they have one up-and-comer (Luke) who currently plays at Texas A&M University.

It's tempting to just chalk this family's athletic prowess to their gene pool. Sure, there is some kind of athletic DNA making its way through the Matthews bloodline. However, let me be the first to stand up and say that having good genes isn't the whole story. It ain't that easy!

Consider the pressures that a legacy like that could produce inside of a young athlete with a family like that. Those pressures can be immense. The children of pro athletes are often supposed to be the best players on the field. Every play, every game, every year. They play with a huge target on their back.

Bruce exemplified the Biblical story many refer to as "the parable of the talents" when he played the game. He took great care to fully realize that with those talents came great responsibility. In Bruce's own words, "God gave the Matthews boys these six-foot-five-inch 315-pound bodies. No doubt those are God's gifts. What I have always been more interested in with my boys is how we will use those gifts to glorify God. I remind Kevin (Tennessee Titans & Carolina Panthers), Jake (Atlanta Falcons), Mike (Miami Dolphins), and Luke (Texas A&M), that we are stewards of these great bodies and the talents that came with them. God's expectation—and ours as parents—is that you do everything with excellence. You should be thankful and generous."

Bruce described how his youngest son battled through his freshman year on the Aggie football team. He said, "Luke went in with the high expectations of being a 'Matthews,' but stumbled at the culture shock of playing for an SEC football program. Coaches getting after him, yelling to get their point across, and putting him in situations where he would get knocked around. He needed to get better, keep his head down and stay the course. I told him that nothing comes easy and he is learning how to be a more humble, hungry athlete."

He continued, "I love that. I like when our kids have to struggle and figure life out on their own. I'm always there as a Dad to offer encouragement and coaching; but, Carrie and I know they have to go through it, own it, and make their own decisions."

Not only is Bruce Matthews a Hall-of-Fame NFL player, more importantly, he and Carrie are All-Pro parents. Bruce continues to bless many families through his work with Search Houston, a group that invites men into the most important conversations about life.

If you really do want to give your son or daughter the best shot at playing a sport at a high level, they must cultivate an unrelenting pursuit of excellence and a strong work ethic. If the Matthews descendants need to learn this, how much more do our children? If they don't, the chances of them playing beyond the high school level are almost zero. If you think they have the talent to play at higher levels, my hope is that you're planting seeds of grittiness for them to fail forward and learn from mistakes rather than falsely propping them up and giving them feedback that is not truthful.

When they fail, talk through it and help them learn from mistakes, but let's not sugar coat the feedback. My sons will tell you that when they stunk it up, I told them they stunk it up; but I didn't leave it there. We talked through it. I always wanted them to walk away feeling better about correcting and improving their performance. We didn't focus on the failure, we focused on the adjustments we'd make after the failure.

This is how we maximize our advantage in the area of sowing and reaping. Great seed planters know what this looks like. We tend those seeds and nurture them over time so we can yield the reward we're after. We pull the weeds and keep the soil rich and nurtured. At the end of the day, then we let God's plan play out with our children. *He* is the Lord of the harvest.

DIG DEEPER

1. Did you grow up in a faith-oriented home? Is there something redeeming you could tell your children about your childhood?
2. What seeds are you planting?
3. How can failure propel future success?
4. If we're only planting seeds for this life, what good is that?
5. Are you honest with your children related to their performance, talent and passion in sports?

6 The Apple Doesn't Fall Far

Have you noticed your children tend to take after you behaviorally? I sure have. And, often, I'm not completely thrilled with this!

The old saying "The apple doesn't fall far from the tree" can be painfully accurate. The tough part for us, as parents, is the bad comes with the good. One of my greatest failures was how my sons saw me. At times, I would disrespect their mother with my harsh words or sharp tone. I've worked on this, and it's taken years to undo terrible behavior toward my sweet bride. Yet, early on, I broke many promises of trying to get better in how I spoke to Christina. I can still struggle in this. Thankfully, through some strong accountability and a lot of prayer and forgiveness, I behave much better today.

My sons saw this as they grew up. We've had some blunt conversations about speaking with the right tone and language, especially around their mom. Christina would ask me to intervene when the boys disrespected her. I admit, I often felt I lacked the authority to correct them since I struggled so badly.

We were probably 15 years into our marriage before I finally said to myself, "Enough!" One day it hit me. I would see and hear my sons behaving the same way toward Christina that I would behave. I felt the shame and thought to myself, "Is this how I want my sons to treat my wife?" Finally, it set in and I knew I needed to make a change.

Partially, I made an intentional decision to improve. But this also came about as a result of my life smashing into the life of a godly man who just wouldn't let me remain as I used to be. Yes, let's talk about Flip Flippen again!

I can divide my life into large sections. There was the time before Jesus came in, and the time after. There's been nothing to compare the difference that Jesus made and how starkly different my "two lives" have been in that regard.

In a similar sense, there was a time period before Flip and then one after him. I've had the great honor to work in his company, Teamalytics, for nearly two decades. This organization has been privileged to help improve leaders in business, sports and our US military. I can illustrate Flip's impact on my life by recounting just one story.

Shortly after I went to work for Flip, he and were heading to an event. As we were driving, Flip casually asked me how my marriage was doing. He said, "On a 1 to 10 with 10 being high, how is it going?" My first reply was, "Flip, that's a really personal question." His response indicated that he didn't seem bothered by my comment. He left me no room to wiggle out.

He said, "Pat, we are not only working together to help *others* grow. I want you to be the best in every area of your life. So, how's it going with Christina? 1 to 10?" Sensing that my deflection strategy wasn't working, I doubled down. I said, "Flip, my marriage is a 9.5. I mean it is really good! Christina and I are good to go." Flip seemed satisfied with my answer and we kept driving. Whew.

About ten minutes later, he asked me for my mobile phone. I thought that was an odd request, but I handed it to him. *What's this guy want with my phone?* He began messing with it. Then, he hits a button and holds the phone up to his ear. *Did he just call someone?* Someone on the other end of the phone answers. Now, I'm getting perturbed. *Who does this guy think he is?* I asked him in as nice a way as you can ask your boss, "What are you doing?"

He waves me off and (*Did he just wave me off?*) I hear him say, "Hi, Christina! Hey, this is Flip calling on Pat's phone. Everything is fine, but I wanted to ask you a quick question. Pat and I were just discussing how things are going in your marriage. So, on a 1-10 with 10 being high, give me a score?" *What in the world?!*

Have you ever been in a situation like this? I can assure you my head was about to pop!

I couldn't believe what this guy was doing. Where did he get the nerve to call *my wife*? I just told him we were at a nine-and-a-HALF! By this point, he could see my cherry red face. He just kept on going with the call. Even so, I figured I was good. I just knew my wife was about to confirm what an incredible, dynamic, perfect husband she'd married.

I could barely overhear her talking through the phone. Alarmingly, her answer was something along these lines, "Well, Flip, it's not great." Flip urges her on, "Not great? Well, give me a score and tell me what is not great about it? You give it a '4' huh? Okay, what makes it a '4?'"

At this point, I am completely ticked off. I can't believe this conversation is actually happening with me sitting right beside my boss! They talk for a few more minutes and then Flip hangs up and hands me the phone.

"Flip, I can't believe you just did that." I'll never forget his reply, "Son, you need to know that you have been blessed with a beautiful, godly woman. I don't much care that she says the marriage is a '4' today. But it won't be '4' next week—or ever again—will it?"

Here's the "best" part. He didn't leave it there. For the next 6 months, every single Friday afternoon I had to call Flip and give him a score. He didn't want my score anymore. I had to relay Christina's score on how I was doing.

That road trip and the following months proved to be a major turning point in my life. I never considered myself a 4 out of 10 in *anything*! I sure wasn't going to be a 4 in my marriage. Since that call, my marriage has had its challenges, but Christina will tell you that whenever it drifted back toward a 4, it didn't stay there long.

How many men have truth-tellers in their lives like a Flip Flippen? I am blessed to say that I have had many more like him, who have spoken truth into my life and held me accountable to a higher standard.

Who are your truth-tellers? Do you have people in your life who have permission to ask the tough questions? Are you transparent in those relationships? If we want to grow, we can't do it on our own. That level of accountability has been a huge blessing for me. I'm still a work in progress and my friends know that there is much work to be done, but with God's help through them, I'm better than I used to be.

Now, I know you may be asking, "Pat, what the heck? I thought this was a book about sports, parenting, and coaching athletes. You pulled a quick one and turned it into a 'How to Fix My Marriage' book." I get it! Stay with me. If you are in the role of coach or parent, who do you *need to be* as a coach or parent? You need to be the best YOU! I could not possibly be the best version of me without men like Flip. There have been many more men and women who have spoken truth into my life. My hope is that you have some Flips too (pun intended).

There's nothing sweeter than a redeemed life. Redemption is the act of saving or being saved from sin, error, or evil. It carries with it the idea of once being unworthy, but then becoming priceless by the grace of God. I'm a product of the redemption of a Heavenly Father. My sons are the product of a redeemed father. I am thankful for God's redemption. Without it, I hate to think of where I would be.

My redemption began in 1989. I was at MLB Spring Training, and it was there I surrendered my life to Jesus Christ. I fully acknowledged the only way to salvation which God offered us was through his Son. That was when I began walking as a redeemed man.

Clearly, a redeemed life doesn't mean we become perfect! It means we now have a way to be saved from sin directly from God. He offers it as a free gift. I'm challenged each day to live the way God wants me to live. My goal is to walk more closely with Him and to reflect a life that honors Him.

Each of us, individually, must be redeemed. It's the only way to gain peace and joy in this life. It's how we move from destructive to productive. From hampered to healthy. As we head in this new direction, albeit imperfectly, we can do something profound. We can take our personal redemption and leverage it for the redemption of something larger than ourselves. This might be our families, our churches, our communities or even our sports teams.

Yes, our sports leagues must be redeemed! We need to not only have redeemed individuals in these leagues, but we also need these same individuals—you and me—to step into roles of leadership and be part of that redemptive process. Let me use my alma mater, Baylor University, as a great example of an organization that has moved in this direction.

Not long ago, Baylor University became embroiled in trouble. A sexual assault scandal rocked the school in 2016, and the university reeled from despicable deeds committed by members of the football team and other students. When the story first broke, I didn't believe it. As some of the news reports were corroborated and the ugly truth came out, I was deeply saddened. Like many, I wondered, "How could this have happened at a school that so positively impacted my life? Where did the train first go off the tracks? How do we get it headed back in a healthy direction?"

What's more, Baylor is a Christ-centered school that is serious about the standards and expectations that a Christian school should uphold. These revelations tore at the core of the institution and its students, staff, faculty and alumni.

Ultimately, the head football coach, athletic director and president of the school stepped down or were let go. The Board of Trustees acted swiftly and made a number of significant changes within the athletic department. To put this in perspective: During the turmoil, more than one hundred employees left the program. Many of these individuals were good, decent people who had nothing to do with the scandal yet lost their jobs. Many were friends of mine. It was a sad and painful time. This was especially true for those individuals who suffered unspeakable pain and trauma. Redemption at Baylor was needed, and my prayer was that God's love would envelope this place and that the victims would receive mercy and justice.

It takes redeemed, whole, healthy people to create redeemed, whole and healthy organizations. And, even then, there are no real guarantees that the individuals involved will be able to redirect an organization as large as a university. However, as we see time and time again in history, even just one key leader can have a tectonic impact.

Baylor ended up with brand new leaders in influential roles who were tasked with a massive reconstruction job. The school needed men and women of integrity and Christlike character to lead it back to a better and more God-honoring place.

I have personally interacted with several of them in recent years. I've met with people like President Linda Livingstone, Athletic Director Mack Rhodes and former head football coach Matt Rhule. I've worked closely with some of them and their staff members on advisory committees. I can say this with all confidence: these individuals are women and men of character and integrity. Their hearts are in alignment with Christ's teachings and values. As Mr. Rhodes likes to say, in the athletic endeavors at Baylor, they intend to "prepare champions for life", not just winners on the field. I believe and support him.

I realize that even godly, gifted leaders like these are human beings. I don't deify them. I give them the same grace and liberty I'd want extended to me if our situations were reversed. There are no perfect leaders. Having said that, I believe they are placed in these key roles for a time and a season to help redeem, restore and repair a broken system. They point to Jesus Christ as their leader and acknowledge that He is the only One we should worship. Praise God that He provides a way back for us individually, and corporately. By almost every measure, the Baylor football program is back on track and I believe will stand as an example of God's redemptive power and grace.

I share this story with you for two reasons. One is personal, the other is broader.

Personally, what does redemption look like in your life? Who do you need to forgive? Have you fully accepted Christ's forgiveness and grace? If the apple doesn't fall far from the tree, how can you set a better example in this area as a parent? Have you seen your own shortcomings "play out" in the lives of your children or the athletes you're coaching? Has your personal redemption been a roadmap for others to follow?

Beyond your personal redemption, how are you affecting the organizations and institutions around you? For the purposes of this book, more specifically, how have you taken your redeemed viewpoint and leveraged it within your children's sports programs? Are you a person of integrity who is actively involved in the shaping of your league or team? Are you "in the game", diving in where women and men of character are needed to lend your voice, help and leadership? Or, are you "sitting on the sidelines", chirping about the many shortcomings and issues with your team, league or coaching staff?

Like the new leaders at Baylor working to redeem their school, involved parents like you and me can do this in our own communities. Once we are—individually—on the path to redemption, we can lean into the organizations we find ourselves a part of in order to help those larger groups become collectively redeemed and productive. Yes, we're imperfect, flawed, and error-prone people. Even so, we can lead well, with God's help and guidance. As we do this, we begin to see how wide of an impact we can have.

I'll never forget listening to a speech from the great Florida State football coach, Bobby Bowden. At an event one day in Houston, Bobby said he loved coaching football because of the responsibility he felt toward his players. He said, "When 70 percent of your players look to you as a father figure, that is a cherished responsibility." For Coach Bowden, coaching went beyond winning football games. He was a truth-teller to hundreds of players, and he made a fatherly impact on those he coached.

So, how does this relate to raising great athletes? Just like the parent-farmer who spends his day nurturing and caring for his crops, if we want our children to live lives of excellence, we must model the right behaviors. If we want our children to honor others, this must start at home. We must honor our spouses. We must treat them with love, respect, and dignity. We must learn to treat others better than ourselves.

Great parenting takes incredible diligence. We're never allowed to "take a day off" when it comes to parenting! It is hard work. If you have been in the parenting game for long, you know how true this is. We must keep our eyes on the prize, the future payoff for all this hard work. If our children follow our (flawed, imperfect) lead, and they choose wisely, it'll all be worth it.

As we see in 3 John 1:4, "I have no greater joy than to hear that my children are walking in the truth." That's a major milestone that we parents look for in our children.

So, if that is the goal, what are the behaviors we need to model for them? Do we want hard working, diligent children? Do we want gritty, get-after-it, confident children? Do we want children with high emotional intelligence? Do we want children who love others and treat people with dignity and respect? Do we want children who love God and show mercy and compassion?

I think most of us parents want all that and even more for our children. Which means we have a ton of responsibility. We must model this well to give our children a picture of what a life like this looks like.

I once had a conversation with a parent of a 17-year-old baseball player. Talent was not his issue; he had loads of it. However, he lacked passion for the game. This player was already committed to a major Division-1 college program, but when the parent asked me my thoughts, I gave them an honest response. "I don't think your son will play much past the collegiate level, if he plays there at all. He definitely has the talent to play professionally, but I don't see the love and passion for the game that's required to play at the next level."

That was a tough message to deliver, but I just believed that in his case, his parents were more passionate about the game than he was. And, their passion wouldn't get him through all the challenges he would eventually face.

Now, I told them that things might change. However, at the time they asked, I had to share that I believed the lack of passion would put a lid on how far he would go. I realized those parents didn't want to hear that. However, I wanted them to see my perspective. As much as I was interested in that young man's sports career, I was more focused on how his lack of passion, zeal, and desire might play out in life for him. His talent could take him to incredible places but going through the motions in life would cause him to regret what could have been.

Passion and ambition are often spoken about in sports (and life) as qualities needed to succeed. I would agree. There is no doubt those aspects are important, but we need to figure out "whose" passion and ambition are driving the player's career. If these get misplaced, they can destroy our relationships with our children.

Our passions and ambitions have risks, especially when those characteristics are pushed upon our children. I wanted my sons to have passion and ambition in whatever sport they chose. But, as their parents, we tried not to push our passions on them. When I was serving as Chaplain for the Houston Aeros Hockey club, Carson became passionate about hockey. The players would cut sticks down and play hallway hockey outside of the locker room with my sons. Of course, they ate it up. The bad news for us was that our sons brought this barbaric sport back home and played incessantly in the hallway of our home! We have the marks on the walls to prove it.

The risk with our passions and ambitions is that if we push them on our children, we can expect them to push back. Any passionate or ambitious person worth their salt would do this! That's an inherent human response. Some children may not push back right away. I've seen some children pushed into a sport for years and they tolerate it. But sooner or later, they push back. Writing in *The Washington Post*, Julianna W. Miner cited the National Alliance for Youth Sports, saying there's ". . . a 70 percent chance your child will stop playing organized sport by the age of 13 because it's just not fun anymore."

If a sport is not their passion, you will end up spending a whole lot of time and resources only to watch it all go down the drain by the time they're 13. Will they have received benefits from playing during that time? Sure, but they have a great risk of leaving a sport behind and placing a high degree of blame on you. That's not a recipe for parenting success.

I believe one of the worst things that can come out of a parent-child relationship is regret or something worse, a child hating their parent for pushing them into something that was not their passion. Christina and I wanted our children to determine which sports they wanted to participate in, if any at all.

Remember, the apple doesn't fall far from the tree. If we're a "pusher of our agenda onto our children," what can we expect them to learn through this experience? We shouldn't be shocked if our children become self-absorbed if we're constantly trying to get them to live "our" lives all over again.

This can be a tough conversation to have with our spouses or children. Many of us had dreams, passions, and ambitions—only to be derailed at some point, and it's tempting to impose those on our children.

I didn't come close to fulfilling my ambitions in baseball. I had it in my mind for over twenty years that I would become the greatest left-handed pitcher of all time. That was my goal, and for a while, it appeared I had a shot at it. Then, I battled arm injuries and found myself struggling just to keep my career alive for years in the minor leagues. Those were hard days, but the passion never left. For most of us, that passion has never left.

Our dreams can't be their dreams. As parents, we need to let our children dream, create their own passions, and develop their own ambitions. Our job is to support and guide them, not live it for them. Mark 12:30 says, "Love the Lord your God with all your heart and with all your soul and with all your mind and with all your strength." (NIV) Our job as parents is to guide our children toward a passion of righteousness which comes from God. If that's the only passion we help our children achieve, then we have accomplished all we need to accomplish.

Flip's company, The Flippen Group, made its name in education. They have become one of the largest teacher-training companies on the planet. His company is a driving force in changing the education landscape of the United States and many other countries around the world. One of Flip's most famous quotes is, "When you capture a child's heart, you capture their head." Said a bit differently, if you don't capture their hearts, you have no business messing with their heads.

There is not a truer statement. I know many educators and coaches feel the same. Every piece of brain research tells us human beings are made to be in relationships with each other. That is how God drew up the plan, and even if you don't agree spiritually, check out the biochemistry of how people think and operate.

We know our brains function through neurotransmitters, or chemicals moving from one nerve ending to receptors at other nerve endings. Some of these chemical messengers are things like dopamine, serotonin, histamine, epinephrine, and norepinephrine. Why is this particularly important in today's culture? A coach, teacher, or mentor has incredible power over the minds of our young people.

And, we tend to reproduce what we are, not what we want. The apple doesn't fall far from the tree.

Research tells us that an adult influence in the life of a child can wield significant lifelong influence. Both positive and negative. This goes for our own children as well as those other children we interact with. I've seen many sports careers propelled by incredible, loving, and caring coaches. I also know many friends who felt their sports careers were damaged severely by an inappropriate, self-focused coach.

When I became a youth coach, my prayer was and continues to be, "Lord, please keep me from ever hurting or damaging a young person. Please deal with me if I were ever to make a youth game about my own selfish ambitions." I came to realize my responsibility as a coach is to lead young people in such a way that I would never be a constraint, that I would help players improve, grow, and develop a passion for their sport.

This is a tremendous responsibility. I have been honored to work with thousands of young people. As I've gotten older, these young men and women have grown into young adults. Funny how that happens.

Now, one of the greatest gifts I get are the messages from former players. I'm seeing many of them get married, start families, and become responsible, community-minded citizens. There is no greater joy than to look back and know that I might've had a small hand in their development. Not only as good athletes, but even as men, husbands, fathers, and servants to others. You will recognize them by their fruits. Yes, we reap what we sow.

In both good and bad ways, the apples don't fall far from the tree.

DIG DEEPER

1. What's one tendency or behavior that each of your children seem to have gotten from you?
2. What's something God helped change in you? Is it something you can share with your children? Do you own the path or is the path owning you?
3. What are your child's passions?
4. How can you support but not push your children toward their passions?
5. What fruits are you seeing in your children? Have you encouraged your children by sharing what you've seen lately?

Bonus Question:

If you are married, ask your spouse, on a scale of 1-10 with 10 being high, how am I doing as your husband/wife? What is something you should change? Who will hold you accountable to that commitment? Don't make me pick up the phone and call your spouse.

SECTION THREE
WORKING THE SOIL

"If anyone is not willing to work, let him not eat."
2 Thessalonians 3:10

CHAPTER 7: The Work is Hard

CHAPTER 8: Enduring the Rainfall

CHAPTER 9: Handling the Sunshine

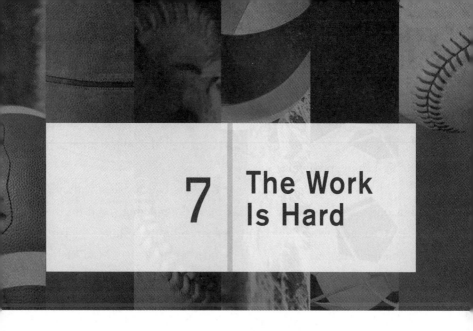

7 The Work Is Hard

Process, process, process. Are you like me, and when you hear that word, it makes you cringe? Why does almost anything good that comes in this world have a process tied to it? Good question, and it's one that will be on my list when I stand before God's throne. Seriously, I appreciate a process, especially if it is one that can easily be duplicated. If it's one like that, I at least have a shot at learning it and putting it into practice. Learning how to pitch is a process and one that I am grateful I was able to learn. That process fed my kids for good while.

An MLB pitcher who was pretty good at mastering process was Nolan Ryan. He was my childhood hero. I had the great privilege of meeting him in 2001. Nolan and I were working with one of the best coaches I have known, Tom House. If you are a baseball fan, you might remember Tom as a former MLB Pitcher and the guy who caught Henry Aaron's record-breaking HR (in the bullpen) in Atlanta. Nolan worked with Tom for the last seven years of his career. He credits Tom with helping to develop a process that allowed Nolan to throw his final Major League fastball at 98 mph, at the age of 47! The all-time strikeout leader in MLB history credits his career lengthening process to Tom and an extremely disciplined approach to his training program.

I'll never forget the stories that Tom and Nolan shared with me, but one stands above the rest. Tom was the pitching coach for the Texas Rangers when Nolan pitched his seventh no-hitter. Nolan's seven no-hitters may be a record that never gets broken. Most Major League pitchers never even sniff a no-hitter during their careers. Nolan's seventh was special for many reasons. First, on the day he pitched it—May 1, 1991—it was his 44th birthday. To hear Nolan's version of the story, he woke up that morning feeling terrible. He even told his wife, Ruth, that he may not be able to take his spot in the rotation later that night against the Toronto Blue Jays.

Nolan made it to the ballpark, took some Advil and headed to the bullpen for his pregame warm up. It didn't last long. He was throwing so poorly that Tom dialed the bullpen phone and called the dugout. He was informing Manager Bobby Valentine that Nolan looked terrible, was feeling bad and may not make the start. After a few more pitches, Nolan walked off the mound and instead of heading towards the dugout, he headed underneath the stands of the ballpark towards the clubhouse. Tom had never seen this happen and didn't know what to make of it. He walked back to the dugout and told Bobby he might want to get another pitcher up and throwing.

The game was a few minutes from start time, but no Nolan. The position players take the field, no Nolan. The National Anthem begins, still no Nolan. Finally, as the anthem finished, Nolan shows up and lets Bobby know there's not much in the tank and he may not get through the first inning. The rest is history. I asked Tom once, "How in the world did Nolan throw a no-hitter, feeling horrible, without even completing his warm-ups in the bullpen?" Tom's response was simple, yet profound.

Tom said, "That night didn't happen by chance. On a night when Nolan thought he might not make it through the first inning, he went back into the clubhouse, sat at his locker and reminded himself about the process. He reminded himself that any Major Leaguer can pitch when they feel good, but he reflected on the reason his training was so intense and disciplined for his entire career, especially these past few years he and I worked together. That process was built for a night like this when nothing was coming together or felt right. Nolan was determined to walk on that mound and give it everything he had, because he relied on that process that we built. It was one that would sustain him through that night and even allow him to pitch three more seasons."

I love that story! Thinking about it gives me the chill bumps. How easily I get caught up in the results and outcomes. Nolan's no-hitter—and Tom's inside baseball story about it—forever changed the way I choose to do life. Especially as I applied it to parenting.

Parenting is all about the process. Those days when I didn't feel my best or when the kids were out of control, I would remind myself, it is all about the process. Just stick to the hard work, the discipline, the focus on what needs to happen in that moment. It doesn't always work in our favor each day. But in the end, the process of becoming a faithful parent, taken one day at a time, will result in a huge win.

Was Nolan frustrated in the bullpen that night in May? You betcha. Was he thinking about a "win?" No way! What was Nolan thinking? Tom said it, "Nolan was just trying to make it from the clubhouse to the dugout." Step by step he made it to the mound and after grinding through the first inning, it all came together. In fact, after that first inning, Nolan came to the bench, looked up and told his teammates, "Boys, all I need is one [run] tonight!"

Working the soil is hard business. Farmers might be the hardest working people on the planet. They have to get a number of things right to raise a great crop. Even when they get their part down pat, there are a ton of uncontrollable variables, which, at any time, can cause disastrous results. The ever-changing weather patterns, insects, quality of the seed, fertilization timing, irrigation and condition of the equipment, all contribute to how effectively the crop will grow. As if those aren't enough wild cards, let's throw in the timing of when you pick the crop and then ensuring it gets safely to a distribution or retail outlet. Don't forget the price-setting that is usually out of the farmers' hands. That's the final step which really determines whether he brings home the bacon or arrives a little light in the wallet.

Did I mention the weather? Yes, I did, but let's talk about it again. Farmers are always battling the elements. They are praying for rain (just enough, not too much); and they're praying for sun (just enough, not too much). They put in decades of learned patterns, months of hard work, and endless hours of praying and hoping, just to see if they can survive to do it all again next year. It's an extensive process, and there are almost no shortcuts.

The work hours are incredibly long, from before dawn until after dusk. Most farmers and their families rarely rest from the time the seed goes into the ground until the time the trucks pull away with the final load. As Cal likes to say, "There is great joy in the morning the day after those trucks leave full." Then, comes the recovery after a long, hard season.

This should be an encouragement and a warning to us parents. Raising godly children is hard work. The reason parenting seems so difficult at times is because, well, it is. And, if we don't fully embrace our "why" for doing it, we'll give up when trying times come.

My "why" for youth sports runs deep. I owe my life to sports. God found me through baseball. When I was a child, my entire being was focused on sports. I played the big three: baseball, football, and basketball. I can hear some of you "insert other sport here" fans grumbling about me not listing your favorite sport as one of the big three. Back when I was a kid, that was just the way it was. Baseball and football are places where I found my identity for many years of my youth. If you came cruising through my neighborhood, you wouldn't find me far from a ballfield. I couldn't get enough.

I treated baseball like a farmer treats his job. I worked at it. For a few summers in my late teen years, I played on four or five different summer teams. I played Big League (Little League for late teens), Connie Mack, American Legion and two different community select teams (the Rebels and Wildcats). I played in three World Series events. For me, a baseball-loving child in Texas, I was living in sports heaven. I looked at baseball fields like a politician looks at county fairs. There were an endless number of them to "work" at any given moment, and I was going to try to hit them all.

I also mowed yards. I started a landscaping business when I was eleven years old. My grandparents allowed me to borrow their equipment with the caveat that I had to mow their yard for no charge. That was a no brainer. Back in the mid-late '70's, I could pull in over

$200 per week just mowing my neighbors' yards. At the peak of my landscaping work, I had about twenty-five customers. I was a lawn-mowing mogul.

My normal summer day consisted of getting up by 6:30AM and working until early afternoon. Then I would drop by my Grandma's house and gobble down whatever she fixed me for lunch. Next, I would rest for a couple of hours and get ready for the big show. Later that day, I would head off to some ballpark and get after it.

The biggest challenge for me was deciding which team I'd play for on any given night. I always had multiple obligations. Thankfully, my coaches were patient with me. There were nights when I would pick up a couple of at-bats or pitch a few innings for one team, and then I would hightail it over to some other field to work the back-half of another team's game. I made baseball my work.

There is no substitute for diligence and perseverance. There's a scripture that serves as a reminder to us as parent-farmers, "If anyone is not willing to work, let him not eat." (2 Thessalonians 3:10). This is a powerful principle for us and our children to follow. On the field, I've heard it said, "Hard work trumps talent, when talent doesn't work hard!" I took my craft seriously and knew I would never look back on it wondering if I had worked hard enough.

Where do our children learn that? Hopefully, it starts at home. Christina and I made a hard decision early in our marriage. We decided to model for our boys that duties around the house were shared. We also decided Christina should work in the home, especially when the boys were school age.

She was involved in school programs, like PTA, and worked as a teacher aide in the elementary schools. She also ran a home-based business to help us supplement income when I was out of baseball and transitioning into full-time work and ministry. I have always worked full-time and at times more than one job to support my family.

My sons saw a dad who worked hard and persevered through tough times. They also saw me make time for them. Clearly, I wasn't perfect at this. But, from the time Carson signed up for youth soccer at age four, I coached my boys in every season at every sport. Well, except for ice hockey. I love that sport, but since I'd never played it, Carson and Conner knew I had little to offer.

I still showed up to practices and hardly ever missed one of their games. Of course, in youth hockey, the little guys get the worst ice time. We had many games on Sunday mornings before church at 4:30AM. Yes, you read that right. I remember lacing up the skates of two little guys who were way too excited to hit the ice at that hour.

I look back on those seasons of life fondly. Our family experience in youth sports was a ton of work. It has also given us some of our greatest memories. There's no denying that if your children get involved in youth sports, it could turn into a huge time commitment. If you're currently living it, you know what I mean. The planning, time, and resources required—they all mount up.

One big variable early on in youth sports: you're just not sure where this sports journey will take you. Some children will experience a tremendous blessing in playing recreational sports. There's so much to learn and enjoy without the pressure to win games and chase trophies. Some will find it to be a dead-end and something they don't enjoy at all.

Our lives quickly focused on select leagues with our sons. There are blessings and curses with where our country has moved in its focus on competition at higher levels. First, it is a ton of time and treasure. I wish someone would have told me I'd need to budget thousands of dollars, thousands of hours, travel across multiple states, and then risk our children's well-being at times—all for youth sports.

That said, we would probably make the same decision today. It was the right call with our boys. But, it would still be nice to know the reality of three sons playing highly competitive youth travel sports for about 20 years. That's a lot of Marriott hotels and Chick-Fil-A sandwiches. At times, we questioned our sanity.

God's Word is clear. We are to count the cost. Luke 14:28, "Suppose one of you wants to build a tower. Won't you first sit down and estimate the cost to see if you have enough money to complete it?" (NIV) If your children are gifted with talent in sports, you will need to decide the best path for developing that talent.

Here is the clearest counsel I can give on this: be prepared to spend way more than anticipated, plan for more time than you can imagine, and then enjoy some of the greatest blessings of traveling with your children. It'll cost a lot of money and time. But, if it's the right fit for your child and your family, you will have some of the best times and create some of the greatest memories you will ever have with your children.

And if your focus is on family time, creating memories, and building character, it all becomes worth it. If your focus is just on the extremely rare likelihood that they'll get that invite to the big leagues, this investment is foolish.

I have so many memories. I would frequently lace my boys' skates at Sugar Land Aeros Ice Center. I can remember the Lamar Little League All-Star games clearly. Youth football in Fort Bend on

Saturday mornings in the Fall became a staple for our entire family. Travel baseball started early for our sons and along the way we created the Lamar Patriots when the boys were in Little League. All of these opportunities were commitments of time and money. They were fun. But, yes, they were a ton of work as well.

Then, our move to Southlake brought us to some serious competition. Our Southlake Dragon youth baseball days were some of the best times for Conner and Casey. We traveled the country playing in VTool Baseball, Perfect Game, and high school tournaments. Conner won a ring playing for the Southlake Carroll High School football state championship team in 2013. Carson's Carroll HS hockey team finished second in the National HS Championships in Chicago, becoming the first team from Texas to make it to the Frozen Four. Casey's Dragon summer baseball teams won multiple National titles. For our family, it was worth every dollar and every minute. We wouldn't change anything.

Clearly, many families can't afford that level of financial and time commitment. That's why the calculation on the front end is vital. Once you get on the highspeed train of select sports, it's tough to jump off. I've seen many parents get sucked in. Many will go into debt or even put their jobs in jeopardy over travel ball. It can get out of hand quickly.

There are many paths to get where your children desire to go in sports. Select ball is not the only answer. I've told many parents, "If your child has talent, they will get discovered." That's not speculation, that's a promise. With all the scouting services and recruiters scouring the country for children who can play, good players get found.

The typical case study goes like this. Your child has athletic talent. You sign them up to play youth ball at the local recreation league.

At ages 5-8, the children start to separate in terms of talent. By the time they're 10 years old, most children know who the standouts are, as well as most parents. Occasionally, you get the overzealous parent with the rose-colored glasses who thinks Johnny is all talent when he's not.

The select organizations are recruiting as early as 7-8 years old. They know who the real players are at that age. You get a call one day that sounds like this, "Hey, I was at the recreation league and saw your kid. Man, can your daughter play! I think she has a real future in softball, and we would like to offer her a position with our all-world, trophy-hunting group of super athletes that kick butt all over the globe. Are you interested?"

Of course, the pride swells when you hear of such an incredible offer. You quickly reply, "Why yes, I'm glad someone finally noticed what a super-hero I have for a kid. Where do we sign up?" Oh, did they mention that the registration fee would cost $2,500, uniforms another $300, and of course, your child's own embroidered equipment is another $650. Last thing, you'll need to cover travel to six of the top tournaments around the country. So, tournament fees, gate fees, hotel, flights, and meals will be another $6,000 for the summer.

For roughly $10,000, your super-kid can become even more super if they play for the greatest-select-travel team on the planet! Now, do the math on your next Little Lebron for ten years and yep, that will be a cool $100,000. Please, and thank you. I didn't even count the lost hours of work production and additional private lessons. Folks, this is not monopoly money, but it might as well be. You'll have burned through a lot of it by the time you get done chasing your little guy or gal around the country playing select sports.

Is it worth it? Honestly, for our family, it was well worth it. For others, you will find no fault in simply saying, "No, not for my family." If your child has athletic talent, you will need to cross that bridge. My final warning is this: it is not an easy bridge to cross. No parent says, "We want the worst for our children." The logic side of our brains would tell us, this select stuff has gone crazy, and logic wins that argument.

The emotional side of our brains will tell us to do whatever it takes to ensure our children develop into the players they dream of becoming. If you have that hotline to God, then you're ahead of the game. Christina and I made a joint decision. We would help our boys develop in youth sports, but we would not go into debt to do it. If we had to get extra jobs to make ends meet, we would do it. And, we did exactly that. We worked hard to provide the opportunity for our children in select ball.

Looking back, it was the right decision for our family. I coached my boys for twenty-two years, in total. I have no idea how many hours we accumulated on the fields, in the hitting cages, in dugouts and as fans during those games. It would be in the thousands. I can honestly say I wouldn't want one of them back. I treasured every single moment grinding through each practice, game, and season. This is because all along the way I knew my boys were developing their character, from the inside out. Since I knew the hours achieved a greater result than just notching more wins, they seemed invested and not spent. I never regretted giving up certain career opportunities that would've netted me more money so I could stay fully engaged in their athletic careers. Deep down, I knew there would be a huge return on that investment.

We were able to realize one of those returns when Conner & Casey both attended East Texas Baptist University and played together for two seasons. Christina and I would say those years were some of the most fun in our family history, and our boys would agree. We got to see them pair up and lead their teams and celebrate big wins and deep home runs. It was fun to watch. All the time, effort, money and travel coalesced in that stretch.

They knew each other so well it almost gave them an unfair advantage. I can recall several times when they were silently in sync on a play that befuddled an opponent. Casey played catcher and Conner was a first baseman. I don't know how many times their brother brains instinctively connected to pick some poor unsuspecting runner off of first base. And I can neither confirm nor deny whether Casey's first college home run was fueled by his brother picking a sign as a baserunner at second base. I am told that a change-up is much easier to hit when you know it's coming. It was hilarious. And, just in case you're a legalist, picking signs as a baserunner is perfectly fine, as long as you're not using video equipment or clanging garbage can lids in the dugout! Moments like those added fun to the mix in ways that we could've never planned for.

There were long hours that we all put in, but our boys were blessed with the talent and showed the passion. They put in the time and effort to improve day in and day out. They did the work of a farmer—from before dawn to after dusk. We, as a family, calculated the cost and found the investments were well worth it.

We saw our share of both rain and sun. But that's for another chapter.

DIG DEEPER

1. As you consider young men and women today, do you think they've lost a sense of discipline, hard work, and perseverance? Why do you think that's happened?

2. If you discover your child has the talent to become the next Lebron James, what responsibility do you have to help them learn to manage that and use it well?

3. Have you calculated the cost of sports, in terms of time and money?

4. Exactly how far are you willing to go to help your child in youth sports?

5. Have you weighed all the costs (money, time, commitment) of youth sports?

8 | Enduring the Rainfall

If you're a 50-something (or older), like me, you remember those incredible television shows from the '70's and '80's. Shows like *Little House on the Prairie, Leave it to Beaver* and *The Partridge Family*. Wow, where have those classics gone? In one episode of *Little House on the Prairie* (the "100 Mile Walk"), it opens with Charles Ingalls holding wheat in his hand. He was staring in amazement at his first crop and raising that wheat to God, saying, "Thank you, Lord!" for his 100+ acres were ready for harvesting.

Later, Charles and his family run the numbers. They estimate they'll clear $2,625 on that wheat. Back in those days, that was like becoming an overnight millionaire. They go to sleep dreaming of what they'll buy with the money. Visions of new boots, dresses for the girls, warm coats and curtains for the window are all dancing in their heads.

That very night, a storm comes. The rain turns to hail and pummels the crop. It's totally destroyed. Every stalk is gone. The next morning, Charles is crushed but he tries to be positive. He tells his wife Caroline it's nothing to be solemn about. He calmly states, "I guess you could say we're back to where we started. It's just one harvest. What's one harvest in a man's life? Nothing."

We suffered pain through youth sports. There's no denying this life truth: where there are people involved, there will be trials. We've seen assaults in the parking lot, parents behaving irrationally, and coaches trying to win at all costs. Even coaches and mentors we trust and believe in will make mistakes.

The father of one of my Little League players was found guilty of murdering his wife. Try coaching through that. The rains definitely came, and at times they poured. Many parents aren't ready for the rain to fall, but some of them are. I've seen some common threads across those parents who are rain-ready.

First, they have the proper perspective about sports. They understand the end game, and they remember that the game is only a game. Also, they seriously consider to whom they will entrust their kids. They look for appropriate, reliable coaches with strong track records. These leaders need to have not only a history of success on the field but off it as well. They must have demonstrated high accountability and integrity in their treatment of players and parents.

Second, they help their children learn life skills first. For these parents, competition is second. This doesn't mean they don't compete hard. Instead, they focus their efforts on surrounding their children with the best influencers and top-notch character models they can find.

Third, these rain-ready parent-farmers don't *dream for* their children, they *dream with* their children. Great parenting involves discovery into their children's hearts and their own motivations.

Finally, the rain-ready parents promote a respect and learning about the game. But, more importantly, they help build great relationships with the team and even with opponents.

One of the great joys of youth sports is dreaming with your children about the gifts, talents, and passions they have for the future. At bedtime, when the boys were young, we would spend time each night reading God's Word through "Bible cards." They were stories from the Bible. The three boys would rotate each night selecting their favorite card. Sometimes, we would read multiple cards. These Bible stories were engrained into our boy's hearts and minds at an early age.

Afterwards, we'd ask them who they wanted to pray for. Christina and I would lead them in prayer. It was a special time. The boys still mention those "bedtime stories" as a difference maker and foundation for how they learned to honor God and relationships. This time would also lead to incredible discussions as the boys grew—conversations about life, dreams, and futures.

My sons, like me when I was young, would lay their heads down on their pillows and dream of playing professional baseball, football, and hockey. They played so many championship games in their dreams. Too many rings to count.

Maybe you can relate. You might've dreamed those same dreams. We can thank the Lord that He authors dreams for us to find, realize and chase. They can be incredible dreams!

Here are some questions I wrestled with as a dad: "Who dreamed those same dreams? Where did they come from? Who is the author? Who, then, is responsible for the talents and gifts our children receive?"

If you trust Jesus, then the answers to these questions are simple. If you don't know Jesus from Donald Duck, then you'll have a different answer. You may not fully believe this, but God is the author of dreams and He can put those dreams into motion.

However, not all dreams come true, do they? Even though God can open those doors, or cause that scout to find you, or give your team a win—it doesn't always work out that way. Some of our dreams aren't granted. Some aren't very God-honoring. Some are just plain crazy and they're not really from God. This can be confusing and difficult to choke down when the rains come. But, one thing we know for sure—the rains will come.

The bigger challenge is how will we handle the rains when they do come?

I recall playing against Cuba in the 1988 World Championship tournament in Italy. The setting sounds exotic, but the game was anything but that. We played in the final championship game against a talented and aggressive Cuban team. We led by a couple runs into the ninth inning, but then, after a controversial call put a Cuban runner on first, they homered to knot it up in the bottom of the ninth. They finally singled in the game-winner and we had to choke down a controversial and difficult loss. What made it worse was their team celebrating in front of our dugout by cheering and waving their national flag. It almost sparked an international incident as we physically restrained several of our teammates from charging them and starting a fight.

Some losses sting more than others. Some dreams die hard deaths. I saw another powerful example of how to handle life's rainfall in the life of my middle son, Conner.

From the first day Conner picked up a ball, we saw talent. He was not the most natural athlete of my three sons. But, early on, he was the most dedicated at working to hone those talents. The passion has always been there. He wanted to be a Major League Baseball player from early in his life.

I wanted to support and help him develop those talents. With God's grace, I encouraged him to be the best baseball player he could be. That said, I had to understand that God was the author of this boy's life. I was not. Armed with that perspective, it made life more enjoyable.

My son received an important benefit in this. I didn't try to live my MLB dreams through him, or my other sons for that matter. Did I do everything I could to help him achieve his dream? You bet I did. Did I support and coach him for thousands of hours of practices and games? Yes! And I enjoyed every second of it! However, we weren't exempt from the rainfall.

We were driving back from a college visit at East Texas Baptist University, where Conner had just committed to play in college. I asked him about his goals. He said, "Dad, I just want to get a chance to play my freshman year and contribute to the team." I challenged him that day to dream bigger. I urged him, "Conner, why not go into ETBU with the goal that you will become the best player ever at that school? That you become a leader on the team, that you lead your teammates closer to Christ? That you break school baseball records? How about a 4.0 GPA? What would hold you back from believing that?" He looked over at me and gave me his signature smirk. I could see the wheels spinning.

Conner went on to become one of the most decorated NCAA players ever. He received 41 awards, including CoSIDA Academic All-American of the Year for two consecutive years. It's only the second time in NCAA history a player received that award two years in a row. He was an overachiever in the classroom as well as on the field. He completed his undergraduate degree and MBA in four years at East Texas Baptist University with a 4.0 combined GPA. He broke a few of those ETBU records along the way as well, becoming the all-time hits leader.

He was an All-American and American Southwest Conference Athlete of the year for two consecutive years. He played collegiate Summer baseball in Ohio and New York and was the MVP of the New York Collegiate League All-Star game in 2015. He spoke with multiple Major League Baseball organizations about playing professionally. He built an incredible resumé during his collegiate career, and all signs pointed to him getting a shot at professional baseball.

The 2017 draft occurred in June as it does every year. His hopes were high, and our family was right there with him. During the draft, he was contacted by multiple teams who told him there was a high likelihood they would draft him. The draft occurred, but no call ever came. We saw the rainclouds forming. He was passed up in the draft and then not offered a free agent contract. His baseball career came to a subtle end. Here came the flood.

Conner deserved a chance at pro ball. But, as I reminded him and did throughout his career, baseball is sometimes a cruel game. The day he decided to quit pursuing a free agent deal and turn to a business career was a rough day. I was angry with the game for not rewarding this young man. He deserved a shot. The rains kept coming.

Conner is a fantastic young man. He busted it for years to be the best baseball player he could be. He chose to attend a college he loved and one where he could play his freshman season.

He started the first game of his freshman year and never came off the field. His teammates chose him to be their team captain his sophomore year. It was the first time in program history a sophomore was voted as Captain. More importantly, he was the spiritual leader of his team. He led hundreds of student athletes in Bible studies all through his time at ETBU. He mentored and led his teammates and other student athletes as a classroom tutor. If any kid earned a shot at professional baseball, it was Conner Combs.

It simply didn't happen.

Here is the coolest part of the story. Conner's perspective was—and always has been—if God's plan included him playing professional baseball, then he would go down that path. And, he would enjoy every second of it. However, if that wasn't part of His plan, he would have to be okay with it. He had full confidence that God had another incredible plan for him.

Did it still hurt when the call never came? Oh man, did it ever! Weathering that storm was no fun. Was it worth it? When you ask Conner that question, he would tell you, "I would never go back and change a thing. I had a chance to play the game I loved through college and had a blast. Some of the greatest moments of my life came during my college years. I am forever thankful God allowed me to play the game at the collegiate level. I am thankful for all the coaches and players I played with. They impacted my life and most of my best friends came from the game. I am incredibly blessed and will always look back on my playing career as a gift from God." The rains can come down and the floods can come up. But God is still God.

Sometimes, the rain is mixed in with the sun. Conner continues to write his own story. From a dad's perspective, looking back, would

I have liked for Conner to play professional baseball? Absolutely. But it was out of my control. I learned to lean on God for peace. God has blessed Conner. He is a leader in so many ways and much of that came as a result of the many years he did get to play the game.

I have many special memories of Conner, but one stands out. As the Captain of his team, he would ask opposing players and coaches if he could bring the teams together after games to pray. Both teams would gather around home plate and Conner would lead them in prayer. Often, this was after hard-fought contests. He never knew this, but my eyes would well up with tears when I saw him on those fields. My son, by God's grace, leading dozens of players in prayer after every series for three seasons? Wow.

Sometimes, we cannot see the why when things don't go our way. I was unbelievably disappointed when Conner wasn't given the chance to play at the next level. For those of us who have played the game at the highest level, we know that's just how it can be. It still didn't make it any easier to choke down.

That was a gut punch. Yet, he moved on quickly because of his perspective. He's now married to an incredible, godly woman, Sarah Rose Summers (Miss USA 2018). They are an awesome couple with a bright future, focused on honoring God in whatever direction He points them. As a dad, I could not be prouder of my son. God has molded him and continues to use him in mighty ways.

When the rains came, I got to see whether my son's character was built to withstand them. I was delighted to find out—it surely was.

As parents of athletes, we have the opportunity to define the perspective of the game. What do we want from it? What do we want from it for our children? This is where priority meets opportunity.

When we go into youth sports with the right perspective, then doors of opportunity will open for our children. The end results could be a college scholarship or an opportunity for the very few to get a shot at professional ball.

For the majority of us, our hopes and dreams should be that our children learn the incredible life skills from the game they will carry with them for the rest of their lives. If we set our sights on forming godly character in them, then even the rains become our ally in this effort.

We can draw closer in our relationship to God through how the chips fall. Whether we win or lose, get the opportunity or don't, we can rely on God to be working in and through us for a greater purpose.

This becomes the bedrock of worthy goals for your family. Then, when the rains come, you'll have built a foundation on the rock that will not get washed away.

I thank God for the rain. If not for the rain, I wouldn't be able to appreciate the sun.

DIG DEEPER

1. What are you planting in your child related to sports?
2. How do you handle dreams for your children? Do you talk about dreams often?
3. What is the proper role in sports for the parent-farmer?
4. How do you handle disappointment in sport?
5. What's one seemingly major disappointment you had as a child—that turned out to be a great life lesson for you? Consider sharing that story with your child.

9 Handling the Sunshine

My youngest son, Casey, has been a solid athlete his entire life. The rest of the family agree he was blessed with pure athletic talent. He is also one of the most instinctual athletes I've ever coached. He is a gritty, never-give-up, hard-nosed player. We saw something special in him by the age of six.

What do you do when you have a talented child? How will you handle success? Sometimes, we fear what'll happen if we have to endure the rain. But, often an equally tough test can be how we deal with the sunshine.

I trust, through the stories and experience I share next, you'll realize some ways to honor God, build others up, and shape your child's influence. As certain as the rain is, we know the sun will also shine. We must be prepared.

We raised our boys when they were young in a community called Pecan Grove in Richmond, Texas. There were neighborhood games every night from football to roller hockey. One late Summer afternoon, Casey came running into the house with his nose bloodied from the neighborhood football game. One of the older boys had "trucked" Casey on his way to what appeared to be a sure touchdown. Of course, Casey hung onto his shirt and dragged him down before he scored, but his nose took the brunt of the hit.

Casey came into the house and his mom screamed. Christina grabbed a towel and began cleaning him up. It didn't take Casey long before he said, "Mom, will you hurry up? I need to get out there for the next play." He didn't care that blood was caked onto his T-shirt. All he cared about was not missing the next play in a neighborhood pick-up game. Dat's-my-boy!

That's how Casey plays the game. It's also how he does life. Casey will figure out a way to beat you or he'll die trying. When you see a player with that healthy passion, almost like a chip on his shoulder, you recognize something different. What should you do if your child has talent? When things are sunny and there's just enough rain and wind, then what?

As his college coach Jared Hood put it, "Casey's the guy you want leading your team into battle. He is one of the most hard-nosed competitors I have ever seen. His will to win is extraordinary and he leads by example. Could he take it too far? Yes, about once per day. It was all I could handle!" Casey's a coach's dream, and occasionally, a pain in the gluteus. But, he's one guy you always want in your dugout.

The risk for Casey comes in the strengths of that hard-nosed, gritty, never-give-up attitude. When he overplays those strengths, they can become liabilities which in our leadership development work we call "constraints". He got this from his dad. Remember the apple and tree chapter?

There were times early in my career when I ticked off my teammates. I didn't know how or when to pull my foot off the pedal. I played the game hard, all the time. Then, when I didn't see the same amount of effort from my teammates, I'd let them know about it. I was not afraid to get in a guy's grill.

That behavior can raise the intensity level on any team. Coaches usually love it (within reason). When it becomes extreme, it can create tension and cause players not to play at their best. I had to learn the hard way when I needed to back off a little and not push so hard. Casey is learning how to do this as well. As I have always told him, "I would rather pull the reigns back on a thoroughbred than have to kick a donkey in its rear."

When we moved to Southlake, it was an easier move for Casey. He was in the fifth grade and made fast friends with a group of athletic children. I was asked to coach a youth football team there. Now, you need to know, one of the most successful high school football programs in the nation is the Southlake Carroll High School Dragons. They have won eight state championships with most coming at the highest level of competition in Texas. Carroll has also won hundreds of championships in multiple sports. Needless to say, expectations are high for sports in that town. It can be tough on everyone, especially the children.

Within a few days of our arrival, I was coaching fifth grade youth football. Thankfully, I was paired with two men who knew the area well. Maury Buford, who played with the NFL Champion Chicago Bears in the 1980's, and Phil Chelf, whose son, Andy, would later play football for Purdue University. I arrived at tryouts in early August of 2007 and was told we could "freeze" five players before the draft. These players couldn't be selected by other coaches. Of course, the other four Southlake teams had already frozen their star players. I relied heavily on Phil and Maury to help select our team.

So, what does a baseball guy do when he needs to draft a football team? Of course, he drafts a bunch of baseball players. That's exactly what I did. We drafted a bunch of good athletes, my son included. I knew if we could draft good athletes, who were smart, we could teach them how to play football. We finished in second place behind the feared "Black" Southlake team that had not lost in four previous seasons.

They also had their core group of "frozen" players that were the best in the league. If ever there was an "unbeatable" dream team in youth football, it was the Black Carroll Dragons team in 2007-08. The next season, I stuck with my five solid players and drafted more students, who had never strapped on a padded football uniform before. Our 2008 team had 11 players, who had never played tackle football. Yet, it was made up of mostly smart, athletic baseball players.

I'll never forget when one of the coaches from the Championship team from the previous season walked over to me after the draft and laughed and said, "Good luck with that bunch! Those baseball kids won't last the entire season." I promise I was gracious months later after the championship game when we beat the famed "Black" Carroll Sixth Grade team.

I later found out parents on the other team had secretly filmed our practices during championship week. Boy, did that make for an even sweeter victory. One gracious opponent's parent found me after the game and congratulated us for the big win. That was one of the most unforgettable seasons in my coaching career.

How in the world did this happen? It started with our first day of practice. We didn't hit the field hard and crush the players to make them tough or call them names for never playing tackle football. We started with a social contract.

We asked the boys how they wanted to be treated by the coaching staff? Then, we asked them how they thought we wanted to be treated? Then, we asked how they wanted to treat each other? We also asked these 12-year old boys how they wanted to work things out when we messed up and mistreated one another?

The social contract became the basis for how our team performed and supported each other. When we messed up with each other (this happened often), we had a simple process to deal with our behaviors and move forward quickly. We also had great leadership from guys such as Casey, Ryan Dykstra, Andy Chelf, Barrett Buford, Nic Motley, Kevin Cramer, Alex Johnston, Brendan Gonzalez and Connor Dickson. Those guys wanted to win, and they formed great relationships.

Casey survived youth football with all his body parts intact. He continued to play football into high school until he hurt his shoulder. He partially tore his labrum on a big tackle. It almost cost him his baseball career. He played with a hurt shoulder for the next two baseball seasons, although he could not play his natural position at catcher. Thankfully, his high school baseball coach moved him to first base, where he became the All-District first baseman his senior year.

Casey had surgery to repair his shoulder after his senior season in anticipation of playing college baseball. He also began delivering pizzas to make some money, while rehabbing his shoulder. I knew he was having a hard time deciding about his future. By the end of the

Summer, he was struggling. He came to me and said, "Dad, I know you're going to be disappointed in me, and I don't want to let you down, but I am going to give up baseball."

My first reaction was shock, but I quickly realized something. He had struggled even in coming to speak with me. My heart was heavy and hurt for him. We would later learn there was much more to the story, but it would be about five months before we figured out what all was going on in this situation.

As a family, we had plenty to celebrate with our sons, who had gone on to play collegiate hockey and baseball. Carson was finishing up his third season at Dallas Baptist and we had a blast watching his hockey games on the weekends throughout the fall. As a parent-farmer, there was plenty of sunshine to go around.

Even amidst this relatively sun-filled season, we had to deal with some tough stuff. Just after the holidays in 2015, we discovered Casey had made some unwise choices. He'd been smoking marijuana with some friends, and it wasn't one isolated case. He came clean and told us he'd been doing it for months. His behavior changed and that original desire to be the best athlete didn't just fade as a result of a bum shoulder. We had seen a change in his demeanor, and it was all beginning to make sense.

He'd given up on his dreams and was content to deliver pizzas and head to community college. It wasn't that pizza delivery or attending a junior college were necessarily bad, but they were stark departures from his recent trajectory. Just a couple of years prior, Casey had dreams of playing college and professional baseball. Those dreams changed all too quickly, and we didn't piece this together until he allowed us a closer look into his world.

Once we knew what we were dealing with, we took two steps that now serve as critical milestones in Casey's life. First, Christina and I hit our knees in intense prayer. We were determined Satan wasn't going to win this battle.

Then, we convened a family meeting and gave Casey just two options. He could join his brother at East Texas Baptist University, or he could live under our roof, where his mom would know his location one hundred percent of the time. She would monitor his every move. Never take her eyes off of him. You're probably picking up the vibe. We made one choice look considerably more attractive than the other.

No self-respecting 19-year-old gives up freedom easily. Nope, not with parents like us. On January 11, 2016, something else happened. Conner, who went back to ETBU to play his Junior season, called to share some breaking news. The team's starting catcher had just gone down with an injury. He wouldn't be able to play in the Spring.

Conner asked for my thoughts about contacting Casey. I suggested he make the call immediately and tell him of the situation, which he did. Things happened quickly. A few minutes after that call, Casey came running down the stairs and told us all about the conversation. His initial response was, "Dad, I thought I was done with baseball, but I miss it. I want to pray and consider going to ETBU to join Conner." That's all his momma needed to hear. She sprang into action, called the university and started figuring out how to get Casey registered.

Within a few days, Casey was on track to join his brother at ETBU and play baseball again. He was still healing from surgery, but by mid-Spring, he could be back to 80-90 percent with some hard work. He jumped at the chance to attend ETBU, and as a freshman, became the starting catcher roughly halfway through the season.

Throughout his freshman season, Casey's life was making a 180-degree course correction. The call from his brother proved to be a major turning point in his life. He'd tell you it was the most important phone call he'd ever received. Even more important than the one he received several years later. That was the one informing him that he was going to get a shot at becoming a professional baseball player. He'd just been selected by the Miami Marlins in the Major League Baseball Draft. Hello again, Sunshine, my old friend!

Casey Combs was ready to give up baseball after high school. He walked onto a Division-3 baseball program and was drafted after his All-American senior season. Casey's story is still being written, but we are now seeing a much brighter path God is opening up for him. He wants to ride the pro baseball train as long and as far as it will take him. He's hoping for a shot at the Big Leagues. If that doesn't happen, I know he'd make a terrific coach one day. He has a plan to coach long after his playing days are over.

The sunshine for us, as parents, comes when we see God at work in our children's lives. We come to understand their giftings and talents. Our role is to encourage, guide, and direct them into those giftings. No, it's not the gifts or talents of your children that make the difference. It's the effort and attitudes your children have toward God's blessings.

The Bible tells us that God resists the proud but gives grace to the humble. It takes humility to acknowledge that we are not the source of our talents and gifts. It also takes humility to recognize we have them. We're not humble when we say, "Oh, I have no talent." We're humble when we say, "Man, I'm grateful that God gave me this ability."

We've seen far too many young people with talent who let it go to waste. Why? It's often because parents were too focused on the talent. They missed the most vital thing, and that was where the talent came from. When we know that, we gladly combine our talents with the key ingredient to maximize them: effort. Dear parent-farmer, if your child has talent that goes to waste, could it be because they haven't heard you say, "I'm glad God gave you that skill. Now, get out there and work your tail off!"

In this age of entitlement, our responsibility is to move our children in the right direction. Toward humility and responsibility, and away from expecting life to always hand them things.

We can make two mistakes when it comes to talent in our children. First, we don't recognize and attribute it to the source: that is God. If we don't see this, shame on us. Second, we see it, but we don't insist on them fully exploring and expanding it. Again, even that is for God's glory, not their own.

It's like that old example of a farmer describing a turtle on a fence post. You know one thing's for sure—the turtle didn't get there by himself! Our kids are not turtles on a fencepost. They didn't get there on their own. The God of this universe is the source of our talent and gifts!

Let's make hay while the sun is shining. The essence of this ties directly into seeing every good and perfect gift that we have as coming from God the Father. And in giving those gifts, He includes a command:

"Each of you should use whatever gift you have received to serve others, as faithful stewards of God's grace in its various forms." (1 Peter 4:10, NIV)

When we have a gift, we are to use it. But, not for ourselves. For Him, and for others.

I've heard many parents talk about how talented their children are (believe me). My question is always, "Great! What are they doing with it?" This might involve crazy ideas like getting our children off their phones and setting them up to excel in those gifts. If we don't help them fully utilize those gifts, then we're failing. I have heard parents say, "Gosh, I don't know how to get Johnny off his phone or video games?" Seriously!? You are the parent. Take the electronics away, if needed. Or, at least put some restrictions on the usage.

"The sunshine has come, but we didn't know what to do with it," some have said. Well, the sun doesn't stay up forever. We have seen the results all around us. It's heartbreaking to see a child with talent floundering, because they lack the resolve, urgency, or intensity to maximize their talents.

May we parents dig in and help our children handle success in ways that honor God, build others up, and shape their influence for Him. May we be diligent to work the soil. Yes, the work is hard, but we must never give up. No matter how much rain falls or how much sun shines. Our guiding principle here is faithfulness. Faithfulness to do the work, no matter the variables. Toiling while understanding it's God who handles the results. After all, if we aren't willing to work, we'll starve. Or, worse, our kids will.

DIG DEEPER

1. What's the sunshine in your life as it relates to your child and sports?
2. Would someone describe your child as entitled or responsible? Or both?
3. How are you currently encouraging your child to work hard?
4. If your teenage children were left to their own devices, would they starve or survive based on their work ethic?
5. If your child works hard, when's the last time you encouraged him or her?

SECTION FOUR

REAPING A HARVEST

*"Then he said to his disciples, 'The harvest is
plentiful, but the laborers are few;
therefore, pray earnestly to the Lord of the harvest
to send out laborers into his harvest.'"*
Matthew 9:37

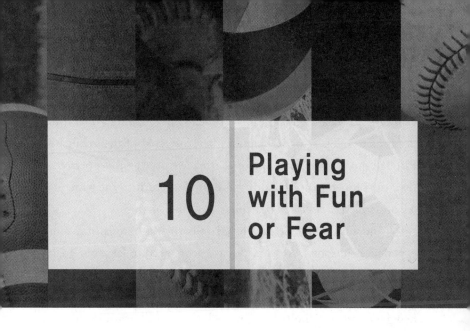

10 Playing with Fun or Fear

Historically, athletic competition has been regarded as entertainment. Only in the 21st century has sport evolved into a full-time, big-money profession. Some major problems with professional sports have surfaced over the years.

There's no doubt that money has changed the game. And, not just at the professional level. It reverberates down all the way to the youth level. The old saying, "Just follow the money," carries a lot of truth in our sports-saturated culture. College scholarships have become like gold, as parents and athletes employ every effort to ensure they win the battle for the "free ride."

As the parent-farmers we are, we can't lose sight of the fun in the journey. It's about the moments in-between games, the road trips themselves, the post-game pizza parties. Our role in some sense is to keep the fun in the game. It's those in-between moments when we have the opportunity to tell stories, pass down wisdom, and laugh together.

The systemic issues of "select" sports are crippling families financially. They're chasing the dreams for their children, but to their own detriment. The parents seeking the "best interests" of their children through sports have gotten out of control. We need a proper perspective, the proper goals of youth sports, and a return to the basic life lessons athletics can teach our children.

I and my family have gathered tons of life lessons from our experiences in sports. As we've discussed, we need to keep our goals focused on growing the character of our sons and daughters. But what happens when we lose sight of this? The game moves from being grounded in fun to being rooted in fear. And, fear-driven missions rarely work out for good.

What are your fears as the parent of an athlete? *Are you afraid your child will get hurt?* If your children play sports, they will get hurt. Usually, it's the garden variety of an injury, like a twisted ankle or bruised shin. But, sometimes, the injuries are severe. That's a risk we all take when we step onto the field. Incidentally, we run that same risk when we drive our car, fly in a plane, or walk down the street.

Are you afraid a coach will hurt your child? That too can happen. I've seen parents entrust their children to the high-talent select coach who has low-character. These are the same parents who are surprised to learn their child was cursed at or abused. Don't let your children play for coaches with shaky character. The game wins aren't worth the personal losses. Don't sacrifice your integrity for coaches who promise to get your kid "looks." If your child is a great player, they will be found.

Are you afraid you will invest thousands of dollars for your child's athletic development, only to be let down when they don't get a college scholarship? Well, that's one fear grounded in quite a bit of statistical truth. Odds are, their athletic investments will not pay off economically. That's just a fact.

You're just about as likely to turn select sports investments into a pro contract as you are to win the lottery. Betting your child will get that coveted scholarship is a huge gamble. The odds are not in your favor. How about lowering that risky proposition and looking at the opportunity for them to leverage their sport to grow their character—no matter how big, small, or nonexistent the scholarship offer? There has to be more we aim to get out of this sports investment than a future financial payoff.

I've seen youth sports deteriorate considerably in the past decade largely due to the dubious "win at all costs" recruitment of elite athletes in college programs. College athletic budgets at the D-1 level now surpass hundreds of millions of dollars, so the war for talent has created a culture of cheating and scandal.

This has rippled down into a sickness that has developed in youth sports. The goal is no longer fun or character-building. No way. Now, the goal is to funnel elite athletes into the college and professional level. The development of select and elite sports tournaments to this end has pushed hundreds of millions of dollars into the pockets of investors. These investors often take advantage of unsuspecting parents who've become swept up into the chase-the-scholarship-dollar tornado.

This high-pressure system has created massive disillusionment for parents and athletes. These parents are now spending thousands of dollars each year to pursue what are most often unattainable goals. The fuel for this system is typically built on lies. We're told our child is the next full-scholarship athlete or professional, and we believe it. What's worse, we write huge checks to see the end of this story, and then we're shocked when it's not the end we'd been promised.

The parent-farmer is a wise steward of their resources, especially time and money. The results for many parents are often far afield from their lie-fueled expectations. Sadly, parents are not only wasting family resources, but expectations are being pushed onto the lives of innocent children. These are the children who desperately need a system that is based on fun, friendship, physical health and character growth. Instead, they get caught up in a combine that will spit them out 10 years later when they're no longer useful for the system's purposes.

The solution to these problems is not for our children to try and figure out. We parents are the adults here, and we need to behave differently. We must get back to the basics of youth sports. Change only occurs when we choose to behave differently. Once our mindset and behavior shift, then, the systems in which we operate will begin to catch up.

I don't blame business leaders for stepping into youth sports. My beef is not with the large national tournaments developed for youth athletics. There is a place and a need for elite athletes to gather and compete at a high level. This competition pushes them to improve. I have partaken in the fruit of elite, travel sport, and still do, as a coach for the Dallas Patriots Baseball organization. My friend Logan Stout and I dedicate our summer and fall weekends to helping elite ballplayers fulfill their dreams of playing at higher levels.

The problem is when we parents buy into a lie. We've let youth sports systems have way too much control over our children's lives.

We have to look ourselves squarely in the eye on this and agree that change will begin with us. We need to remove the fear-based underpinnings of our youth sports pursuits and replace them with the fun-infused elements that make them what they used to be.

With our Patriot teams, it starts with the goal. Our goal first is to build up men of God who take their baseball talents and leverage them to gain education and skills beyond the game. Occasionally, we have the opportunity to coach players like Trevor Story, Josh Bell and Chris Davis. These are each former Patriots who went on to enjoy All-Star Major League careers. But Logan and I are just as excited to see players move on to tremendous college careers and become incredible future husbands, dads and community leaders. That is why we coach!

Many children are no longer competing for fun and to learn great life skills. They've become tools for parents and coaches to seek after personal fame and fortune. Simply look at the results of what is happening in the culture of youth sports. This attitude of "winning at all costs" is producing disastrous results in our children. Many of the most talented are being shopped around for play on "super-teams" of All-Stars from around the country. The reason? To win the biggest showcase tournaments for the glory of the team owners and coaches. And, don't think for one minute there isn't big money involved in those transactions for teenage players.

I want to reiterate a statistic mentioned earlier. By the age of thirteen, 70 percent of children drop out of organized sports. The incidences of abuse on playing fields has risen exponentially, as coaches and officials are being cursed at and threatened. These heightened emotions have led to outright violence and abuse. Children are overspecializing in specific sports at younger and younger ages. Orthopedic doctors have documented an alarming five-fold increase in injuries to joints, muscles, and tendons to children over the past two decades*.

I hope that you and I can band together and deliver a change in youth sports. We need a wake-up call and we need to understand that the root causes are only the beginning. We must deal with our expectations surrounding our children as they relate to life on and off the field.

Many of us have unrealistic expectations for our children and we've allowed these expectations to drag us away from the core principles that should undergird our youth sports programs. Even so, there is hope. We can step in and bring the fun back, and like other positive changes that occur in a society, it starts with the behaviors we teach and tolerate.

We need more parent-farmers to nurture and guide these young athletes well. We need engaged moms and dads who see youth sports for what they can and should be. We need you.

Matthew 9:37-38 says, "The harvest is plentiful, but the laborers are few; therefore, pray earnestly to the Lord of the harvest to send out laborers into his harvest." In a real sense, the harvest of youth sports is plentiful. But, the character-led laborers are few.

On the bright side, I've seen some efforts to improve education and outcomes as it relates to parents and coaches. There are great

---

*Landro, Laura, *The Wall Street Journal*. "For Young Athletes, Injuries Need Special Care.". January 6, 2014. *https://www.wsj.com/articles/ no-headline-available-1389026936*

programs at our fingertips. We can type in an online search and find a video training for any need out there. And, training will definitely be a piece of the solution, but it's not enough.

What we need is systemic change. Change from the ground up. Change that cannot be ignored, squashed or stopped. How does that usually happen? Almost always, massive change begins with strong leadership and accountability. And, in this case, I'm not talking about tournament organizers or league officials (only). I'm talking about us. The parent-farmers who push those around them and their children toward a better way.

So, what should be our goal? What is the goal for our children and what is the goal for us as parents? I have learned through watching youth sports that we can never underestimate what God is up to with these young men and women. He has a path designed for them.

I've worked with children in youth sports who came into a sport with little ability but with an armload of desire and passion. Once they learned the skills, their athletic careers took off. These children excelled. I've also seen athletes come into a league with a ton of skill and all the potential in the world. And guess what? Those skilled children often slowly fade away, or "behave" their way right out of the game.

We don't know what God has in store for our young athletes. They may be the next Wayne Gretzky, Michael Jordan, or Tom Brady. Or, they may play recreation ball for a few years and have the time of their lives, but their skills don't translate to higher levels of competition.

Whatever the case, parents and coaches need to realize something: we don't control their future. God does. We're called to help our children steward the talents they have been blessed with. We exist to encourage them to live out their dreams and desires in a godly manner.

As parents, what then is our responsibility? Ephesians 5:1 says it well, "Follow God's example, therefore, as dearly loved children." We are invited into a personal relationship with a God who loves us, and who wants us to be more like Him. That's it. We need to keep God and His plan at the center of our athletic pursuits.

We know the responsibility we have as parents. And true to his character, God hasn't left us alone to figure it out. When we know Him, He gives us His Holy Spirit. The Spirit leads and guides us. If we live and act in accordance with God's Spirit, He promises to show us how to experience an abundant life. I know, this can be easy to write about but a challenge to actually live out.

It's one of the reasons we have the church! God provides others who are trying to live and act in accordance with God's leading, since He knew we couldn't do it all on our own. God adopts us and then provides a great family to surround us.

Christina and I would not be at this place in life without our church family. My life would be far different, had it not been for strong, godly, relationships with other men who held me account-able in tough times. Most of these men came across my path through sports, church, or in parachurch ministry. God saw to it that I would have the chance to learn at the feet of these incredible men. Of course, I had to make that choice, but I can't imagine where my life would be without those who spoke God's truth into me.

The fun for me, as a dad and husband, comes in how these rela-tionships have led to an abundant life. I want to serve God with all my heart, abide in Him, and lead others to live, love, and lead like Jesus. That is fun and challenging. It also carries over into how I lived my baseball career.

I played with a ton of passion. I wanted to be the best I could be in every phase of my career. I wanted to be the best player, the best teammate, and the best leader. I didn't do it perfectly. But my desire was to play the game right. I knew the talent God gave me was a gift. I also knew with that talent came a huge responsibility.

Most of all, I wanted to have fun and enjoy the journey.

My mom taught me a lot about how to live with joy. I wish you could meet her. I don't know anyone else in the world who has been through as much junk as she has but continues to model passion and joy every day.

There is an old saying, "Don't let anything steal your joy." She has never allowed anything to steal her joy. Her joy is contagious. Thankfully, she's passed this joy down to her children and grandchildren. MeMa simply won't let you put your head down for long.

This is a defining characteristic of every high-performing athlete and it's one that relates directly to raising successful children. We need to teach, model, and live our lives with joy. I believe this is what a follower of God looks like—that no matter what the circumstance, no matter how difficult life gets, no matter what negativity enters into your life, you live with joy. We want to model a life lived with a joy that transcends circumstances, scoreboards and scholarship offers.

Our Savior, Jesus, was hanging on a cross with nails through his hands and feet for an offense he didn't commit. Even so, what was His response toward the people who killed him? He said, "Father, forgive them, for they do not know what they are doing" (Luke 23:34, NIV). Who does that!? Only a man who's fully wrapped in joy can do this. One who's walking in forgiveness and grace. Jesus modeled that for us, and he wants us to live with joy.

This is the precise gift we're offered through God's Son. The gift of joy.

From my perspective, that's how we can live and play the game with fun instead of fear. We can tap into the God of this universe, follow Him, love Him, and live for others to see Jesus in us. Christina and I have been through some difficult times. I'm sure you have too. Your life and our lives are a collection of stories. Some good, some tragic. The key to keeping the fun in this life, and in our youth sports leagues, is understanding that God is in charge of writing those stories. We just need to walk after Him and seek to do His will.

My parents wrote a lot of my story when I was young. I have had many influencers who wrote parts of my story along the way as well. It took me a while to recognize that God was in charge of writing my story. I simply chose to follow Him with joy. That's what I want to pass along to my sons and their families. That's how we'll impact the world and leave a godly legacy. We will live a life that points to God.

We did this in sports with our children by celebrating victories and also celebrating the tough times. Our lives did not center around the next win or loss on the athletic field. Our perspective was always to celebrate victories and learn from the losses. We knew that loss and difficulty "produce endurance, endurance produces proven character, and proven character produces hope. This hope will not disappoint us, because God's love has been poured out in our hearts through the Holy Spirit who was given to us" (Romans 5:3-5, CSB).

That's how we can consider "losses" a blessing. God never allows a loss to go unused, if we understand it from the perspective of learning, developing, and growing from those challenges. That is how we can take the fear out of this life. We know a loving God who is walking beside us, no matter the circumstance or what we've gotten ourselves into. He will never forsake us and that comes with a holy promise.

It's super fun when you realize God is in control of the game. All of a sudden, the wins look different and the losses don't sting as badly. We see, not perfectly, but with purpose. We learn to take in the moments of fear and fun, to pass down our stories to those around us. We can laugh and cry together. And we do all of this out of fun instead of fear.

DIG DEEPER

1. Does your child play sports out of fear or fun? Explain.
2. Did you play sports out of fear or fun? Is there a story you can relate to your child here?
3. When can you count a loss as a blessing?
4. What's been your biggest "victory" to date?
5. How do you celebrate the victories?

11 Yielding a Bumper Crop

Yielding a bumper crop happens when we stay committed to a process. When we focus on character wins, our children win. When our focus shifts to winning a sporting contest, our children tend to struggle.

We want our children to be responsible, loving, compassionate, and diligent. These character traits are the real wins. After all the games are over, we want to see that the sport has developed a character in our children that prepares them for real life. We want to know that the wins and losses have combined to help our kids be ready for the future.

Our family decided we would compete hard in every contest. We wanted to win every game we played. But, the conversations after the game were focused on how we loved our teammates and how we behaved, especially when something didn't go our way. We talked about responsibility, honoring coaches, working hard every play, playing with passion, and respecting the officials.

We allowed sports to be an important part of our family. At the same time, we fought the urge to allow sports to define our lives. Biblically, one key responsibility we have with our children is to teach them the pitfall of gaining the whole world while losing our souls. We wanted our children to learn, grow, and use the skills they discovered through sports to build their character.

Our oldest son, Carson, enjoyed a college hockey career. Which is rather ironic. It's hard to believe any child in Texas, especially back in the early 1990's, would want to play hockey. We had some of the greatest street hockey games in history. They'll go down as Greater Houston area sports lore. Most of the children on our block would join us for those evening games. If you can picture a 6-foot-4-inch, 220-pound grown man playing street hockey with professional hockey players and a bunch of children skating around, that was our street most evenings.

This may shock you, but my roller hockey career came to an abrupt end one evening. In the process of trying to avoid one of my sons skating by me, I jammed my stick into the curb. The trouble was that the other end of the stick was pointing toward my groin area. Laugh if you want, but it wasn't funny at the time. I thought it would require a trip to the hospital. Thankfully, an ice bag and some rest did the trick. And, my wife and I weren't planning on having any more children, so no harm, no foul. I can say that now.

Looking back, if some discomfort and swelling was the price I had to pay to see where hockey would take Carson, it was worth it. That sport gave him a terrific opportunity to grow and experience incredible accomplishments in life. He's the oldest of our three sons. He was an absolute pain in the rear between the ages of 3 and 18. Yes, that whole time. He pressed us hard to see what all he could get away with. He viewed his brothers as competition. And during most of his years in our home, he was as manipulative as he could be.

Today, he's hard-driven and entrepreneurial. He's also a loving and caring man with a tremendous passion for life. Carson's life turned around when he was a college sophomore. That was when he figured out life was not all about him. There have been a couple of life-changing moments. One happened at age 11.

He was playing youth football and he suffered a terrible knee injury, especially for a boy his age. I'd been on an adjacent field, coaching his brother. One of his coaches ran to me after a play. Carson had been buckled underneath another player. There was a loud pop. My son was on the ground in an awkward position and it was clear he had suffered a significant injury. There was immediate swelling and by the time we got him home, the knee was in really bad shape and he couldn't move it.

We took him to the doctor the next day, who told us we'd need to wait a few days for the swelling to go down so he could do an MRI exam to see the extent of the damage. He put Carson on crutches and prescribed ice treatments and anti-inflammatory medications. After a week, the MRI showed a torn meniscus in a couple of places. It was a rough injury.

The meniscus had worked its way into the joint, which was what was keeping him from being able to bend his knee properly. The orthopedic surgeon we were seeing had performed surgeries on multiple professional athletes. He told us that it was highly unusual to see an eleven-year-old with a torn meniscus of this magnitude.

He was reluctant to perform surgery, but he felt if he could repair the cartilage at Carson's age, then he would be able to resume athletics within a year, after some intense rehabilitation. We were hopeful, but not entirely optimistic. It was devastating news.

During this stretch, we were attending a couples' Bible study at Sugar Creek Church. Christina immediately informed the other moms what had happened, and the prayer alert sped out. The surgery was scheduled. Carson went under the knife the very next week.

Christina and I waited in the recovery room for a long time, but I couldn't stand sitting there waiting. I left to grab a cup of coffee. After 15 minutes, Christina called me back to recovery. The surgeon was with her as I walked in. The doctor had a stunned look on his face and my heart sank. I assumed something had gone terribly wrong.

He sat us down and laid out a series of pictures of Carson's knee. As he stumbled through his words, he told us he normally didn't perform surgeries on 11-year-old children. He seemed to say this apologetically, as if it might explain what he would tell us next.

He showed us the MRI again. He compared the MRI with the other pictures. Then, he explained that when he and the staff got inside Carson's knee, they saw a normal knee. There was no meniscus tear. There was no scarring or damage at all. He said that right after he got inside the knee, he gave the nurses a confused look. He thought they had opened up the wrong knee.

He again showed us the conclusive pictures from the MRI and gave us this assessment, "Mr. & Mrs. Combs, I have no other explanation than to tell you that in the time between the MRI and today, your son's knee has been healed."

Christina and I were floored. She started crying as I began high fiving the doctor. Then, he said something I'll never forget. He asked us, "I'm just wondering if you believe in the power of prayer?" We said yes and that our church had been praying for him. He said, "That's the only viable explanation I can offer to you." He then asked for our permission to share Carson's MRI with other orthopedic doctors at conferences as a case study. I told him, "Sure, doc, as long as you give God the credit."

The story gets even more strange or more interesting, depending on your faith persuasion. I was sitting in the recovery room waiting for Carson to come out of the fog of anesthesia. After about 30 minutes, he began to wake up. The nurse approached the bed. Carson leaned up and without hesitation, told me, "Dad, I told you I was fine, there is nothing wrong with my knee." I got up and walked closer to his bed, glanced up at the nurse, and asked if she heard what he said. She nodded in agreement. I asked him to repeat himself. He was sound asleep.

Carson was released from the hospital that day and within a few hours, he was walking almost entirely normally. He's never had an issue with that knee again.

Now, I grew up in a traditional church. We rarely attended, but we dropped in on major holidays. When Christina and I were married, we both decided to follow God and joined a church in Houston. If this was God's way of teaching us that He has power to heal, and that He can use circumstances to move people nearer to Him, it worked. This incident played a role in Carson drawing closer to God. He played hockey through high school. Then, he was about to hang up the skates but decided to play at Dallas Baptist University (DBU).

Those 3 years at DBU were a huge turning point in his life. It was there he met Dr. Blair Blackburn.

During Carson's Senior year, his brother Conner was attending East Texas Baptist University (ETBU) in Marshall, Texas. Conner was playing baseball. After Conner's freshman year, the president's position at ETBU opened up. I met Dr. Blackburn at a DBU baseball game, where we became friends. I was praying about the open position one day. During my prayer, I felt God directing me to call Blair about it. Blair had been the Vice President at DBU for many years. I thought there was no way he'd consider leaving for ETBU.

I've learned that when God prompts me, I need to listen. I made the call asking Blair if I could pray for him and I casually mentioned the ETBU president's role. Little did I know, Dr. Blackburn had been contacted by ETBU about the position and he and his wife, Michele, were praying about it. A few weeks later, Blair called to tell me he'd accepted the ETBU president's position. And, he wanted me to consider joining him on the Board of Trustees.

Again, that's just how God works. Within a few months of Blair taking the ETBU job, he called to ask if he could talk with Carson about an idea. I gladly agreed and asked him what he wanted to propose. He said he wanted to bring ice hockey to East Texas Baptist University, and he wanted Carson to start the program.

I told Blair, "Please forgive me if I sound a bit shocked, but how do you think a 23-year-old, fresh out of undergrad, can come to Marshall, Texas, and help you build an ice hockey program?" He laughed and told me, "You know better. It's not just Carson; it will be God and me walking this out with him. We cannot fail!"

Every time I recall that story I get choked up. Here's the deal. I love my son and I know he has that entrepreneurial fire, but if I'm completely honest, I had my doubts about how this would play out. He'd been in a job for less than one year in Dallas and was kind of floundering. Then, here comes this call from the new President of a University in East Texas asking him to consider building a collegiate hockey program from scratch. After the initial call with Dr. Blackburn, Carson figured there was no way a hockey program could work in East Texas.

Not only that, the time frame was extremely compressed. He got the call in March of 2016 and that would only leave him about four months to create a schedule, order uniforms, and find at least 20 players to fill jerseys! Their season would open that Fall. I don't know how many college sports programs you've launched from scratch, but even if your answer is "zero," you know this sounds impossible.

Dr. Blackburn called Carson back and asked to meet with him in Marshall, TX. Carson reluctantly took the meeting, knowing the task given by Blair would be almost impossible to pull off. During the meeting, Carson agreed to pray about it. I also encouraged him to seek God and not move until he'd heard clearly from Him. I had processed the risks and was skeptical. I wasn't necessarily doubting Carson's ability to pull it off. But I knew the timeframe was not doing him any favors, and I wondered if he could get it off the ground that quickly and not disappoint people who were counting on him. After a few days, Carson felt that God was telling him to trust Him and that he needed to give this hockey program a shot.

Carson launched the ETBU hockey program in April of 2016 and by early July, he had four players committed to play for them as part of the Texas Collegiate Hockey Conference. If you know any-thing about hockey, a typical roster consists of about 25 players. Car-son was working hard to find anyone who could skate, breathe, and who wanted to take a chance on playing ice hockey at a brand-new program. All this in a state not exactly known for its winter sports activity, if you know what I'm saying.

He made a few adjustments to his recruiting practices, hit his knees in prayer, and by the start of school in August, Carson filled out a roster of 17 players and two goalies. He had a team. They also put together a winning season in their first year of competition. A minor miracle in the world of collegiate hockey!

In just their third overall season, the Tigers finished second in conference play and won their first post-season game. In this most recent season at the writing of this book (2020), the ETBU hockey team is nationally ranked in just their fourth season of play! Carson did a great job of finding players in many ways, one of which was through help from some great relationships he built through Hockey Ministries International. He brought players in from all over the world: places like Canada, Sweden and many from the northeast and upper Midwest United States.

It's been remarkable to see what God, Carson, Dr. Blair Black-burn, Ryan Erwin, Coach Alain Savage, Skyler Spiller and many oth-ers have accomplished with ETBU Hockey. This was yet another faith-deepening experience for me and my family. Maybe you've heard that with God all things are possible. Even ice hockey at a D-3 school in East Texas.

I share that to reinforce a key point: The crop we are after is character-based. It's a crop that we sometimes won't see come to maturity until our children are faced with a challenge. A big challenge like the one Carson faced. We then get to watch the character crop come up out of the ground, as our kids rise to the occasion and overcome adversity, doubts and the odds being stacked against them.

We're just hitting that season in our life where our grown sons are starting to make adult choices and take on bigger life challenges. And, now that we're on the "other side" of youth sports, we look back on the many reasons we involved ourselves so heavily in those activities. We are seeing the fruit of those labors, even as I'm typing the words of this book.

It's hard to accurately measure the yield we have received. All of that time and money has reaped an incredible crop. The blessings have far outweighed the cost, pain and lack of sleep. As we're seeing, the biggest wins are the wins in life. Our boys have had incredible coaches, developed life-long relationships, and come out on top of many athletic contests.

However, the most valuable gain has been watching how God has used sports—and the challenges sports threw at them—to draw them near to Him. He also used those same things to draw our family and extended family closer together.

We are starting to see the tremendous bumper crop God has produced in our lives from sports. We're grateful that our children were able to experience many of these benefits.

I can't help but think of the Scripture, "Now to Him who is able to do exceedingly abundantly above all that we ask or think, according to the power that works in us, to Him be glory in the church by Christ Jesus to all generations, forever and ever. Amen" (Ephesians 3:20-21, NKJV).

As parent-farmers, we want our children to be responsible, loving, compassionate, and diligent. These character traits are the real wins. After all of the games are over and the money and time have been invested, we'll be wondering about the return on all that investment. Did sports really help our children get prepared for real life? Did those trials help your future leader be faithful?

We need to diligently look for these often-unseen fruits. Frequently, they show up after the games are done being played. So many leaders in our country come from athletic backgrounds. In a world that is in desperate need for godly leadership, will we parent-farmers be willing to focus on growing these young men and women to serve our world in greater capacities?

This leads us to the greatest question for us, as parent-farmers: What difference would it make if parents saw their own children as divinely appointed mission fields?

DIG DEEPER

1. What's the real-life win for your child related to sports?
2. Would you consider yourself a faithful parent?
3. Would your child describe you as faithful?
4. How has a trial helped you become a more faithful leader?
5. When was the most recent loss your child experienced? Can you talk about a life lesson from that failure?

12 The Farming Never Ends

If you're a mom or dad, you know the farming never ends. My parents told me long ago that even when our children leave home, they always come back. They may not come back to live here forever, but they're never fully "gone." And, for that, we're grateful.

The relationships will hopefully continue long into adulthood. My parents had that right. Now, I'd like to address a key question for you to consider. I've saved this extremely important question for the final chapter. It carries the most significance, due to the consequences that endure beyond this world.

As parent-farmers, how much time are we spending on the temporal versus the eternal? If you are a person of faith, you know that in the eternal context, everything we do matters. That question we posed at the end of the previous chapter takes on even more meaning. What if we looked at the mission-field implications of our roles as parents? We are taking part in developing young men and women who will then become missionaries for God in a world that so desperately needs them. That's a powerful thought.

Long after the balls stop bouncing and the innings end, we want life-long friendships with our children. We want them to know God. And, we want to continue pointing them to Him even after they've left our homes (and we've changed the locks).

Just as the farming never ends, the game of parenting never ends either. Sure, our role should shift from coach to friend, but that's when the fruit of our work really pays off. That's the crop which keeps on feeding us forever.

Think about all the time, effort, and money we're putting into our children. Especially as it relates to their life in sports. Yet, at some point, we know it'll end. Some finish sooner than others, but even the best athletic careers come to an end.

What will we have left after the game?

Hopefully, one thing we have is a great memory book filled with incredible wins in life on and off the field. Ideally, we'll also have a ton of relationships that last for a lifetime.

These benefits are incredible. However, every one of these benefits is also temporal. We cannot and will not take them with us when we leave this place called earth. In comparison to the time, effort, and money we're investing in the temporal, how much time and effort are we providing our children when it comes to the eternal? Are we spending time on the things that matter most? The things that will matter beyond this life? How are we doing at pointing our children toward God? Are we praying with them and for them? Are we teaching them the biblical ethics, morals, and laws that will pay off forever? Are we attending church and becoming involved with a community of believers? Are we discipling our children and helping them to connect with other Godly leaders?

If we're focused on what life can bring to us in the here and now, I'm convinced we will live unfulfilled lives. I was around hundreds of individuals in pro baseball. Many of them look back with some degree of regret. Their lives were focused on the temporal. Most of them did not consider an eternal perspective of life. So many of my former teammates and coaches have seen lives filled with destruction woven through their families, fortunes and fame.

As parent-farmers and coaches, we must resist this temptation. We need to push against the urge to focus on the things of this world that in the long run don't really matter. We need to be intentional about the things that will impact lives and leave this world a better place.

My boys make me look sharper than I really am. They're strong young men. Whenever I'm asked how my wife and I raised them to turn out like they have, my best answer is this: by God's grace, our family focused things in such a way that could encourage, build, teach, mentor, and train up our boys with an approach that pointed to God. We held Him up as the perfect standard, not ourselves.

Recently, I asked my son Conner what it means to be a "Combs." His reply was, "to follow Jesus with all our hearts, minds and soul. To treat others with dignity and respect. To live out lives that shine the light of Christ and draw others to him." Nailed it. Thank you, God, that we didn't entirely get in the way of your amazing grace.

To help us put this into action, we developed a list of "non-negotiables" that I believe helped us keep these principles in place as we raised our boys. These are our Combs family non-negotiables:

1. Love God with all our heart, mind, and soul.
2. Treat others with respect and dignity, and love them beyond their faults.
3. Honor your family: God first, then family, then everything else.
4. When making a decision, always think about how that decision will impact your relationship with God and your relationships with others.
5. Don't be dumb. But, if you do something dumb, don't cover it up. The tangled web always gets messy.
6. Life is tough and we will go through pain. Lean on those who love us, seek wisdom from the wise, and grind through it. God will use it.
7. Be generous.

It's not a complicated list, and you can probably build one that's more elegant or effective. And, no, we don't have these printed out and stuck on our refrigerator. Instead, Christina and I chose to live these principles with our sons. As a parent-farmer, it's crucial that we keep the right perspectives with our children. Christina and I never set a goal to raise "perfect children who do no wrong and make us look good."

That may look strange when typed out, but we've been surrounded by people with those exact expectations (often). Which is crazy, because we all know that goal will never be reached. We are sinners. Our children are sinners. So, we're all going to sin. In fact, some of us are extremely good at it.

We combine this tendency to sin with this age of broken psychological approaches to parenting that instill a lack of accountability and discipline among our children. It's a disaster. I think most of us can agree that the soft "feel good" approach to parenting has not and will not produce excellence in our children. Without strong accountability, our children will fail to fulfill their God-given potential.

One of the greatest lessons we can teach our children, especially through sports, is to get outside of themselves. We have seen this massive movement toward self and self-fulfillment become the overriding thought in mainstream society. It's nauseating.

Look around at any group of middle-school or high-school students today and see what they're doing? They're looking down at those little screens, stuck in their own little worlds. They're not paying one ounce of attention to what's going on around them. What has this social media-fueled era produced? I would argue it's producing the most narcissistic generation we've ever seen. How do we combat this evil? One way is to get them into sports—for the right reasons—and get those phones out of their hands.

As we're doing this, we can also promote activities that require our children to serve others. If we want well-rounded, emotionally intelligent children, we should look for opportunities inside and outside of sports to get them connected with other people. These are situations where they need to deal with real people who have real conversations.

One of the ways our family accomplished this was to engage in mission activities. We chose to involve ourselves with numerous missions and local ministry groups over the years. We have worked alongside organizations like the Fellowship of Christian Athletes, Athletes in Action, Unlimited Potential Inc. (UPI), Focus on the Family, All Pro Dad, Manhood Journey, Search Ministries, Children's Hunger

Fund, Samaritan's Purse, local food pantries, and other ministries that care for those in need. These are other-people-focused efforts.

Our boys learned at an early age that serving others brings immense joy and blessing. For our family, it fulfilled the need to serve God and others. And, it helped to keep the focus off ourselves.

In 2015, our family became more focused on how God could use us to make a difference internationally. Our family now takes an annual mission trip to Belize. Our goal is to help reestablish baseball in that country. The country moved away from organized baseball in the mid 1970's due to budgetary constraints within the education system. Our family is helping to bring baseball back to the country and it's a joy to watch it happen!

With some incredible relationships through one of our Pastors, Omar Reyes, and Jermaine Crawford, a godly leader in the Belize education system, we will see the first Little League season in Belize launch during the spring of 2020. Tom Roy is my mentor at UPI. He taught me that we are telling the greatest story ever told (the Gospel of Jesus) through the greatest game ever played (baseball, of course).

When we first traveled to Belize, it was an eye-opener for our children. I'll never forget seeing my youngest son, Casey, get emotional during our first trip to Belize City. There were tears of joy when we unpacked the 1,000 pounds of equipment and uniforms for the children. It was like Christmas in July.

Then, there were tears of sorrow when our sons recognized many of the children had arrived at the clinic with no shoes and barely a piece of decent clothing. Jermaine let us know that we needed to follow his protocol for providing for the children. He's required to keep a close inventory on all equipment. He told us that we brought incredible blessings to the country, but that he would need to keep track and take possession of the equipment from the children at the end of each practice. If the children returned home with the uniforms and baseball gear, it would most likely be taken and sold.

As heartbreaking as that was to hear, the mission trip put into perspective just how blessed we are. My personal goal is to share that mission experience with as many families as possible. If you want your children to get outside of themselves, then provide them opportunities to serve others. It's a life-changer.

Now, you don't have to leave the country to do this. We have seen poverty-stricken neighborhoods in American cities that have started to use sports as a way to revitalize their communities. You probably have a place where you can help within an hour's drive.

Regardless of how you choose to direct your family members to think outside themselves and even outside of just your time here on this earth, I hope you'll do it. Do something that gives your children a wider perspective on how they can serve and a longer time horizon than even their own lifetimes.

I hope that some of our stories will provide you and your family ideas to get started. I hope you're inspired. We all understand that parenting, like farming, is tough work. The blessings, though, are too many to count when we dive into it with all our best effort.

We will experience a tremendous amount of sunshine, and maybe have more than our fair share of rainfall to go with it. As I look back on the storms we weathered, I'm grateful. It was during those storms that our family learned to rally together and hit our knees in prayer. It was in those moments that God seemed to teach us our greatest life lessons.

As we've broken through to the other side of parenting and we're nearing that empty nest phase, we've come to a significant realization: God's law of sowing and reaping cannot really be hijacked. We either plant good seeds and find the rewards of a blessed harvest; or, we plant bad seeds, and endure the pain of reaping difficulty and strife.

That's one law that just won't be tricked. It'll be in effect whether we like it or not. We get what we have planted; we get it later; and, we get more of it. When my buddy Cal plants carrots, he gets more carrots.

When we plant those seeds of discipline, hard work, determination, and perseverance, we will have the opportunity to see those seeds grow into incredible fruit. Christina and I celebrate every day that our boys got it right in those areas. Generally speaking, they work their tails off and don't expect anything to come easy. They've chosen, for the most part, to live their lives in contrast to the culture around them. For that, I am most thankful. We rejoice when they are loving God, seeking to honor Him, and are living on mission.

The harvest always comes later than when we plant it. And, frequently, much later than we want it to! I enjoy the phone calls I get from Cal during their harvest season. That's when all his family's hard work, sweat, prayers, and tears have paid off. He's upbeat and thankful during those times.

I once asked him if he can predict how each season will go when that seed goes in the ground. He thought a bit and said, "There are so many variables, even before the seed is planted. I really have no idea how each season will play out. Farming is hard! You find out very quickly that most of what we do to create a great harvest is out of our control." For those of us with grown children, we know exactly what Cal means.

There is a great reward to be gathered. You're probably like me, and you want your family to have a positive impact on the world. And, you realize that we have some incredible opportunities ahead of us to do just that. We want to live differently than the self-absorbed society around us. We seek to focus on the things that will last beyond this life. We strive to be parents who seek God first and honor the Creator with our children. Of all the things we're given to steward, the lives of our children are the ones that carry the most weight.

As much as Christina and I would like to take credit for three sons who are a tremendous blessing, we cannot. We give all the glory for that to God. We know that it's only through His grace and blessing that we can have any positive impact on our children or this world. Long after the balls stop bouncing and the innings are over, we want to point our children to God.

Our hope is that our children will ultimately point others to God as well. When you've stewarded those child-raising years well, those children give you back an adulthood that's nourishing and rewarding.

May God help us be disciple-making parents, parent-farmers who look forward not only to the harvests in this life, but in the life to come.

May we live out Matthew 9:37-38, "The harvest is plentiful, but the laborers are few; therefore, pray earnestly to the Lord of the harvest to send out laborers into his harvest." May you and I realize that it's His field we get to work and His fruit we get to gather in. May we put our hand to the plow and joyfully work both day and night. May we cultivate the crop well.

Above all, may we be found faithful to God.

John 15:11 says it this way, "These things I have spoken to you, that my joy may be in you, and that your joy may be full." I pray your joy will be complete as the Lord of the harvest blesses you with more than you can ask or imagine.

There's a reward waiting for us.

There's a future out there worth more than any score.

It's harvest time.

DIG DEEPER

1. How much time are you spending on the temporal versus the eternal?
2. How would your child answer question #1?
3. What are your family's non-negotiables? Have you discussed your family's non-negotiables with your spouse and children?
4. Are you living a life of full joy?
5. Would your child describe you as living with joy? Why or why not?

THE FINAL EXAM

Yes, there will be a test. And, fortunately, you've already started taking it. At the end of each chapter, I shared "Digging Deeper" questions. I hope you took them seriously and thought about your answers along the way.

One of my mentors is Bob Tiede. Bob has dedicated his life to teaching others that leadership is not always about having the best answers or solution. It involves asking the right questions. His books about asking questions are some of the best business development books I have read. Bob saw this manuscript as I was developing it, and he told me how proud he was that I have included no less than 340 questions in this book. Wow! I didn't realize there were that many!

Hopefully, those questions have caused you to pause and take inventory. To think more deeply. Most importantly, I hope they've spurred you on to specific changes in areas you need to address. They caused me to do the same.

I don't know about you, but those words "Final Exam" would cause immediate anxiety when I was in school. I'm hoping I didn't cause you to panic with the title of this section. But, what good would a class be without a "Final Exam" to bring out the best in us?

So, brace for impact. Let's walk through one final set of questions. These are the Top 10 most important questions for us to ask. Half of them are questions we should pose to our children. The other half are ones that they should be asking us. Even if you're putting them in front of players on your team and not your own children, they'll work great. Are you feeling brave?

From Parents or Coaches to Children:

1. On a scale of 1 to 10 (10 being best), how am I doing as your parent (or coach)?
2. What is one specific thing I can start doing to be a better mom or dad (or coach)?
3. What is one thing you want me to stop doing?
4. What is one thing you want your coaches to know that would help them coach you better?
5. What is your goal in sports and how can I best help you to grow toward that goal?

From Children to Parents or Coaches:

1. What do you (mom, dad, coach) like best about me?
2. What is one thing you want me to do more of?
3. What is one thing you want me to do less of?
4. What is one behavior that I can improve upon which would make me a better athlete?
5. Is there something you see in me that could be a constraint in me fulfilling my goals and dreams?

EXTRA INNINGS

If you picked up this book and made it this far, my hunch is that you and I would enjoy grabbing coffee together. You're a parent who wants the best for your child or children or a coach who feels the same way about your players. You understand that parenting and coaching can be tough, but you've already made—and you'll continue making—big sacrifices for your children and players if it sets them up to have a blessed life. You're in this for the long haul. You know what kind of harvest you want, and you're out there every day working the fields. In some cases, literally!

Well, if this is you, I would like to share a scripture verse in closing that means a lot to me. It's from Paul's letter to the Galatians. Early in this letter, Paul acknowledges a key thing about the people in this region to whom he is writing. He notes in the first chapter that the Galatians are under attack. They have people preaching a false gospel to them and it's throwing them into confusion (Galatians 1:6-7). These are people who've begun walking on the right road, but forces are acting on them to cause them to turn away or head back.

Paul wants to help them know that there is fruit ahead, if only they stay the course. He caps off this letter of exhortation and encouragement with this gem in the final chapter:

> *Let us not become weary in doing good, for at the proper time we will reap a harvest if we do not give up.* —**Galatians 6:9 (NIV)**

I'd like to end this book in similar fashion. I'm standing "on the other side" of more than two decades of leading my family through the exhilarating gauntlet of various levels of athletics. From the moment they first learned to play catch in the front yard to the recent years of scholarships and draft day jitters, I've seen it all.

Here's the promise: if you properly utilize sports for their best and highest use, that is, to help children develop character, you'll find a blessing on the other side. If you become deceived into believing that youth sports are your ticket to financial freedom or your outlet for unrestrained anger, you'll have a miserable time during and after their athletic endeavors. And let me double-down on that last point. If you leverage sports incorrectly, you run the risk of losing your children to the unseen spiritual forces that are out to destroy them. The battle is real.

Agree with me that you'll use sports as the character-building tool that it is best designed to be. You'll never regret it, and if you don't give up, you'll reap a harvest; and, it will be a family that loves, challenges and supports one another. And, even better than that, LORD willing, it'll be a family that loves God with all their hearts, soul, mind and strength.

Don't give up. Harvest time is almost here.

ACKNOWLEDGMENTS

There are so many people to thank for writing these stories into my life. I'm most grateful to God for using those people and stories to shape this pot of clay into a man.

Thanks to my friends and family. I would not be near the man without your help! My parents, Dennis & Claudia; Mother-in-law, Paula; my sisters & brother, Madaline, Jackie, and Dennis Jr.; and, Maria, a cousin who is like a sister.

To my friends and mentors, who have invested so much in me. There is nothing on earth that I could give to repay you for speaking truth into my life. I could never repay you. Many thanks to Lee Bason, Fenton Moorhead, Paul Hicks, Matt Barnhill, Steve Kreloff, Philip Petscher, Mickey Weston, Tom Roy, Bob Roberts, Omar Reyes, John Tolson, Jeff Thomas, Bill Arp (in memoriam), Jeff Barrett, Ed Young Sr., Patrick Kelley, General Robert Van Antwerp, Richard Blackaby, JohnAden, Jim Denison, and Vince Nauss.

To my English teacher at Alief Hastings High School, Marilyn Arehart: you must be smiling at the prospect of this guy writing a book! You planted great seed more than three decades ago.

ACKNOWLEDGMENTS

This book doesn't happen without the encouragement and help from my dear friend, Kent Evans, of Manhood Journey. I'll never forget the conversation in the Austin airport. "Kent, I have a great book idea for you. You need to write this book to help parents of youth athletes." After about 5 minutes into the conversation, he stopped me and said, "No, Pat, *you* need to write this book!" Ryan Sanders, you are a most awesome editor. Appreciate and love you guys! Thank you, Paul Byrd, for seeing the potential of a life-long relationship when you introduced me to Kent.

You're not a father on accident.
So, go be a Father On Purpose.

What would it mean to your family if you were a father who lived fully *on purpose*? Imagine waking up every day with a gleam in your eye and a spring in your step, ready to lead confidently and intentionally. This can be you.

However, this world is working against you. Endless distractions, temptations and lies from our enemy combine to make us completely exhausted. We tap out and forfeit as a dad. We raise the white flag and surrender. It's easier just to keep our heads down and put in our hours on the job than to fight the good fight at home every day.

Father On Purpose can help you get back in the game. This is a community of dads who want to raise godly children in a rough and tumble world. To do this, we band together. We learn from one another so we can discover what works well, and what doesn't.

Being a dad is too important to go it alone.

Come join us.

www.fatheronpurpose.org

We Help Dads Disciple Their Sons.

Are you a father of sons between the ages of 8 and 18? If you are, you're in a battle. A spiritual battle for the hearts and minds of your boys is raging. Know why? Because they're the fathers of tomorrow.

One of the greatest legacies you can leave this world are godly fathers coming right behind you. In many ways, it's the greatest earthly hope this world has. Men who can love and lead their families well.

Manhood Journey exists to help you intentionally disciple your boys. We provide resources—Bible studies, eBooks, reading plans and digital courses—to help you faithfully lead and prepare your young men for an adulthood that will honor God. You may not feel like you have the tools, training or qualifications to be a future-godly-father-maker.

We can help you get there.

Learn more: **www.manhoodjourney.org**